Margaret Rutherford

ALSO BY DAWN LANGLEY SIMMONS

Me Papoose Sitter
Peter Jumping Horse
Peter Jumping Horse at the Stampede
Osceola
Vinnie Ream-the Girl Who Sculptured Lincoln
A Rose for Mrs. Lincoln
William the Silent
All for Love

Margaret Rutherford

A Blithe Spirit

BY HER ADOPTED DAUGHTER

Dawn Langley Simmons

McGraw-Hill Book Company

New York • St. Louis • San Francisco
Toronto • Hamburg • Mexico

1 2 3 4 5 6 7 8 9 F G R F G R 8 7 6 5 4 3

ISBN 0-07-057479-0

LIBRARY OF CONGRESS CATALOGING IN PUBLICATION DATA

Simmons, Dawn Langley.
Margaret Rutherford: a blithe spirit.
1. Rutherford, Margaret, Dame, 1892-   . 2. Actors
—Great Britain—Biography. I. Title.
PN2598.R8S56   1983   792'.028'0924 [B]   83-5382
ISBN 0-07-057479-0

Book design by Grace Markman.

For
Gwen Robyns
and
Sybil Tannenbaum

· Contents ·

But there is more latitude in eccentrics. They are always honest, and have their own quality of madness. In the final assessment, I think they will be the saints.

Dame Margaret Rutherford, O.B.E.

Margaret and Stringer's wedding photograph, March 26, 1945.
(Rutherford House.)

· Author's Preface ·

MOTHER RUTHERFORD and Father Stringer were the only true parents I ever knew, for they gave me the love and security of being wanted in a real family.

They staunchly defended me and stood firmly by my side during my greatest personal crisis, when others I had deeply loved and helped in many ways were sadly lacking.

The Rutherford-Davis home on Packhorse Road, Gerrards Cross, remains in my heart as an oasis of delight in a busy world. There at Elm Close, with its fairy snowdrop ring, my father personally cooked our wedding breakfast, serving it on the best Rockingham china. Many happy hours were spent tucked up happily under Aunt Bessie's old carriage rug in the chimney corner, while my mother read her favorite Mary Wilson poems aloud.

After Mother was gone and I stood outside in the street with my father, the dear house no longer ours, he suddenly gripped my arm and exclaimed as if in consolation: "Well, at least your mother would have liked the new gate."

The present owners have been very kind. They have even invited my young daughter, Natasha Manigault, to play on the lawn!

If Vita Sackville-West is smiling benignly in heaven at what happened to me, she has a perfect right to do so, for I became a real live Orlando and not a fictional one as she had been.

Born Gordon Langley Hall in Sussex, England, in 1937, I spent all of my vacations at Sissinghurst, where Vita Sackville-West and her diplomat-writer husband, Harold Nicolson, began reading my little writings when I was four. Vita told me always to be realistic and never say for instance, "Clean as a new pin"—for whoever heard of anybody washing a pin? Harold ordered me to go into my writing room at ten every morning, apply my bottom to the seat of a chair, and work until lunch, after which I was to go into the garden and weed or do something equally useful. This is a pattern I have diligently followed all my life. I have never had time to smoke, drink liquor, or take drugs.

My natural father, Jack Copper, was officially Vita's chauffeur, but his duties included buying her dogs and carving their tombstones, creating a garden seat from bits of marble taken from an old Tudor fireplace, and winding the clock in the towers. Marjorie, his wife and my natural mother, was beautiful, educated, well-versed in the classics and, as Vita once told me, "could tell a splendid story, had a wicked sense of humor, and should have been a writer." Marjorie hated Sissinghurst; it was her prison, something that Vita never did understand, although with that certain British flare for class distinction, she once admitted that "poor Mrs. Copper had married beneath her." Marjorie was more of a sister to me than a mother.

I always wanted my natural father to love me but, being partial to baby girls, he hated me. He never took me upon his knee and played with me as he did my sister; he took pains to tell me I would never be *anybody,* which only gave me more incentive to prove that I would.

Fortunately, I was raised by my half-Spanish grandmother, Nelly Hall Ticehurst, who with her identical twin sister, Aunty Doom, an antiques authority, had in their youth been pioneer women bicyclists and had then married brothers. My grandmother's husband, Arch, had been killed one Christmas Eve in a tragic accident when he was only thirty-six.

Mum, as I called her, had a green thumb; although she could never see a weed, she always managed to produce more flowers than Lottie Lambourn, her precise and perfect horticulturist neighbor. She hated housework and once a year sold everything except her piano to Ted Errey, the used-furniture man, and bought new. She spent most of her time clipping newspapers and making notes. My own child, Natasha, asked me the other day why I was always clipping the paper before she had read it. The reply came naturally: "I've been clipping all of my life."

Unfortunately, I was the family black sheep in more ways than one: Marjorie, still unwed, had borne me when she was sixteen, in those days very much the unforgiveable sin, although she did later marry my natural father. Her pregnancy was, to say the least, horrible. Shunned by most of her family (her Baptist aunt, Elsie Ticehurst, told her that she was "a disgrace to virginhood" and that she hoped she never lived to see another of her nieces in her "condition"), Marjorie locked herself in a darkened room for most of the nine months. One close and sadistic relative saw fit to kick her in the stomach, which she always believed had something to do with my own subsequent sexual condition. It has given me some satisfaction to know that in his old age he has been stricken with prostate trouble.

When I was eventually born at home with only a midwife in attendance, the clitoris was so swollen that the startled woman did not know whether I was a boy or a girl. In Britain in those days, when in doubt, the child was automatically registered as a boy, often with dire results later. Years later, in a scientific article, *Gender Is a Moot Point,* published in the *London Daily Telegraph* magazine, writer Wendy Cooper would tell how such unfortunate things happened back then. Today it would be put right almost immediately, for most babies are born in hospital. For example, in 1982, a so-called boy-child was flown to the United States from its native Haiti for corrective surgery so that it could grow up in its true feminine gender.

To me it was a catastrophe, for the deformity was so noticeable where it mattered that I could not even use the public washroom facilities like the other boys at the Church of England school. Luckily I lived close to home. I looked like a little girl, I liked to play with dolls, and when it came time for my voice to break like all the other choirboys', of course it refused to oblige me. Then when I was between twelve and fourteen there were irregular bleedings that were, close relatives told me, "to be bravely borne but in secret. Think of the disgrace and laughingstock you would be to all of us if anyone ever found out."

Little wonder that I lived in the stories that I wrote. There I could always be the heroine, fearing nobody, perpetually looking for her fairy prince. Besides, there were always holidays at Sissinghurst to look forward to, in spite of Jack Copper. There, where eccentricities were perfectly normal, I did not feel so out of place. Vita Sackville-West dressed like a man in her riding breeches and big Spanish hats. Even as children we knew that "that terrible Mrs. Woolf" (Virginia Woolf) had had a lesbian affair with Vita and had written a novel about her called *Orlando,* in which over the years "he" turns into a beautiful woman. The photographs at the end of the book, which I managed to find at the Public Library, were clearly of Vita. I remember that it gave me courage; as my grandmother used to repeat so often, "It will all come right in the end"—as indeed it did.

My grandmother died at home of cancer. I helped nurse her with my mother, Marjorie, for whom I always felt a gentle love. After that, life was grim, as nobody wanted me. I ended up in an attic room without even a teakettle. It was like something out of Dickens. I remember jumping on my bicycle and riding up to Heathfield churchyard, throwing myself down in the snow across Grandmother's new grave, and weeping uncontrollably.

Shortly afterward, with what little money I had saved and some insurance money from my grandmother, I took off to Canada. I crewcut my hair and decided that even if I knew I was a woman, nobody else did, and I would have to make the best of it. I felt I was a vegetable; I could have no close friendships, for I had no real sexual feelings for either men or women. I wound up as an uncertified teacher on an isolated Ojibway Indian reservation on the shores of Lake Nipigon, where, when I wasn't teaching or cooking the school lunch, I was making notes for future writings. Out of that unique experience came *Me Papoose Sitter,* which was a gratifying success (in 1981 it was chosen as one of the best humor books during the last twenty years and republished in a famous Danish collection), and several juveniles. My books on Indians were always sympathetic toward them, and surprisingly popular with members of the tribe.

A few years later I managed to get to New York City, where I believed that if I wanted to be a professional writer, I had to live like one. I worked as an editor with a newspaper syndicate and wrote *Me Papoose Sitter* at night. The morning that I was ready to take it personally to the publisher T. Y. Crowell to read, I hadn't the price of a subway token. I walked the twenty-two blocks with the manuscript under my arm. Bill Poole, the editor, read it and bought it. It was later also published by Hutchinsons' in London and in several other foreign countries, and shared as a dual Books Abridged Bookclub selection with President John F. Kennedy's *Profiles in Courage*. British movie star Anthony Dawson optioned it for a film. Sex or no sex, at least I was on my way!

Unfortunately, I soon became sick again, swelling up in the abdomen and bleeding internally. I lay in a New York hospital until a distant cousin (we were related by an Anglo-American marriage) found me. She was Isabel Lydia Whitney, America's first woman fresco painter and a watercolorist of merit. Asking why I had not let her know that I was living in the city, I replied quite truthfully that I wanted to see if I could sell my first book on its own merit and not because of the illustrious Whitney name. She went home impressed and a few days later announced that since she was living alone in a forty-room mansion on West Tenth Street, she would like me to have the entire suite of eight rooms on the top floor. Well-meaning friends were always worrying her to move into an apartment, but she had been used to big houses all her life. Number Twelve was her home; all she asked was to be able to live out her life and eventually die there. If I were living in the same house, we could be company for each other and yet retain our individual independence. We would meet every day for tea and spend Sunday afternoons and evenings together. She knew about my affliction and thought that the Whitney home would give me protection and a sense of belonging. She was then a lady in her seventies.

As a young woman, Isabel had received a proposal of marriage from a man often described as the richest in the world—Calouste Sarkis Gulbenkian, whose art collection now fills the great Gulbenkian Museum in Lisbon, Portugal. She had refused his hand because her only sister, Hasseltine, had said that his surname reminded her of oranges! Years later when he was elderly, I met Mr. Gulbenkian at the Old Bailey when I was covering a murder trial for the *New York Post.* He was carrying his lunch in a little brown paper box. Of Isabel he said then: "She had the most brilliant mind I ever found in a woman. It was like a jeweled comet."

I spent six happy years with Isabel, during which time we did not have a single unhappy word. During that time I wrote several biographies, including those of Baby Doe Tabor, the Silver Queen of Colorado, and Vinnie Ream, the Girl Who Sculptured Lincoln. The latter, a book for young adults, made history of sorts on Madison Avenue where it was chosen as an adult bookclub selection.

It was during this time that Margaret Rutherford and Stringer Davis first came into my life. She had been given a copy of *Me Papoose Sitter,* which she began to read while sitting on top of a double-decker bus, becoming so interested in the contents that she wound up in the garage with the bus for the night. She was then about sixty-eight years old and at the peak of her acting career; Stringer was seven years younger. Eager to play the role of an old Ojibway lady, Poor Old Grandmother, in a proposed movie of my book, she came with her husband to visit us in New York. There Isabel told her of my medical condition, and something of which I was not then aware, that she was in the first stages of terminal leukemia.

Margaret and Stringer, who had married too late in life to have children, had recently acquired a lovely home in Buckinghamshire, Elm Close. Their hearts were touched and they asked me to join their family. "You will have a real home to come to in England," they said. I realize now that Mother, as I called her from that day, knew only too well the burden of carrying a grim family secret in her own life. Her generous

soul could envisage the great weight that mine had been . . .
and even then, still was.

I stayed with Isabel until she died, quietly and with dignity,
in the museum-like home she loved. It was I who closed her
eyes, and with the help of Joan Crawford, a personal friend,
arranged her funeral. At her request she was buried in England beside my grandmother, Nelly Hall Ticehurst. Isabel's distant cousin, John Hay Whitney, then the American
Ambassador in London, helped with the arrangements at
that end. He went out of his way to be compassionate and
helpful.

From then on I spent part of each year at Elm Close, and
the rest in an old pink stucco mansion that I had bought in
Charleston, South Carolina, the Dr. Joseph Johnson House,
Fifty-six Society Street. It was the first house I had ever
owned and I poured my heart into it. I had earned quite a lot
of money from my writings and Isabel had left me very well
off indeed. I had also inherited her New York real estate.

Life in Charleston seemed charmed; there in my walled
garden I could write and dream. Then fate took a hand; I
became violently ill with more bleeding and was rushed by a
frightened housekeeper to Roper Hospital. The nurse assigned to me was Mary Kaye Hardee, a fine Catholic mother.
She recently told Dena Crane, who was preparing a documentary on my life, that "I went to Gordon Langley Hall's
room, pulled back the sheet and had the shock of my life.
There lay a beautiful woman."

The rest is history. Simple surgery put my life into its true
orbit. The doctors seemed most concerned that my mind
would not stand up to the drastic change from male to fe-
male. After months of periodic visits to a women's clinic,
where I was told that in matters of sex I had the mind of a
fourteen-year-old, I was cautioned that if I ever married, I
needed somebody of great understanding who would give
me the peace of mind that had for so long been denied me.

Unfortunately, the human heart does not always listen to good advice.

Back in Charleston (where I had been received with open arms into local society, because of my credentials as a successful writer and as first the adopted son and then daughter of Margaret Rutherford), the dowagers soon recovered from their titters of amusement concerning the fact that I was now known as Dawn Pepita Hall. In fact, they were looking for some quiet, settled bachelor among their exalted ranks to whom I might be safely and properly wed. Nobody could see all that money and a mansion full of Whitney family heirlooms going to waste. What they did not know was that all my life I had been a born romantic . . . the fictional men in my life had all been of the *Jane Eyre* "Mr. Edward Rochester" kind.

Little wonder that the first man in my life was, to say the least, somewhat out of the ordinary. He was married to a nymphomaniac who kept her lover living in a tent in their garden. Not only did he look uncommonly like Burt Reynolds, he was very much the aristocrat and gentleman. We had what seemed to me much in common—a love for plants, birds, antiques, and Margaret Rutherford movies. Even Mr. James, the butler, enjoyed his visits, and he did *not* approve of everybody.

How all this would have ended I do not know. My cook, Irene, had a date with a young man named Simmons, who failed to show up on time. She left for the night in a huff and when the doorbell rang a few minutes later, I opened it to see John-Paul Simmons, then a young motor mechanic with dreams of becoming a sculptor. His black hand touched my white one; it was simple as that. Next day he crashed into the house, having bought a pail-full of flowers in the marketplace, tripping and literally showering me with them.

Back in England, Mother was recovering from a broken hip and far from well. My subsequent engagement and marriage put her and Father back on center stage again. Father had complained before of how quiet life had become and that nobody ever came to see them. Now my engagement photograph was stolen from a silver frame in my Charleston drawing room on Tuesday and appeared the following Sunday on the front page of London's *News of the World* under the headline ROYAL BIOGRAPHER TO MARRY HER BUTLER.

To make a long story short: the gentleman whose wife kept her lover in a tent never forgave me . . . *Newsweek* said that I had shaken the *Cradle of the Confederacy* . . . and John-Paul and I were married in my sitting room, after the church where the wedding was to have taken place was threatened with bombing. It was the first legal mixed marriage in the state of South Carolina.

The reprisals were terrible: A firebomb thrown at the crates containing our wedding gifts from England nearly burned us and our elderly neighbor, Catherine Theresa Salmonsen, in our beds. Through the sheer chicanery of some of Charleston's so-called white society people, I lost the mansion, which nearly broke my heart. We had twelve hours to vacate it; the works of art and antiques were piled up on the porch. We moved to a derelict house on Thomas Street.

Three years later, after Natasha was born, a local antiques dealer, Suellen Austin, came to warn me to leave Charleston—that a contract had been placed on my life. Years afterward Albert Goldman, author of *Elvis,* taping for Dena Crane's documentary, told her that I had not stood a chance, that certain members of Charleston society had employed the Mafia to exterminate me, a fact he had discovered while investigating the link between the Mafia and drug-trafficking in that port city.

They nearly did exterminate me. The night of Suellen's visit I heard a crash upstairs in the old broken-down house where I was then living. Going to investigate, I found a white man holding a knife over the baby. He broke my left arm (crippling it for life), a shoulder, my nose, and two toes, before throwing me off a third-story porch. Miraculously, I survived and the baby was safe. Nothing had been taken from the house. My purse lay untouched on the dining room table!

Natasha Margienell Manigault Simmons had been born on my birthday, October 16, 1971. Dr. Elliott Phipps, a prominent Harley Street specialist, had told me that I could have children of my own, when Mother, hurt by sensational tabloid stories channeled out of Charleston, took me to see him, along with a representative from one of London's Sunday newspapers, *The People*.

During the long months of pregnancy the paparazzi pursued me unmercifully. Cameras were placed high up on the porch of the Old High School opposite our home. Pictures showing me taking John-Paul's lunchbox down to the docks, where he worked for a time, were flashed around the world. As Larry Shelton, Charleston's leading beautician, told Dena Crane: "Dawn was then as pregnant as anybody could be."

After the attack on me and my baby, John-Paul, Natasha, and I fled to the small mountain village of Catskill, New York—where, with my home and money gone, he promptly deserted us, throwing the key in my face. He ran off with a woman who had shot and killed her first husband; she was older than I. We didn't see him again for ten months, during which time she forged my signature to a document: all my antiques and paintings in storage in Charleston were sold at auction without my prior knowledge. With John-Paul's help, I was now wiped out financially.

John-Paul was later found, himself deserted, living in a cellar in Albany, New York, selling his blood to survive. It was midwinter, with snow on the ground. His mind had been permanently ruined by drugs and alcohol.

Meanwhile, Natasha and I began what were the unhappiest few years of our lives. I taught art in a Catholic school (which Natasha would later attend), wrote articles and, with what I earned, got us a home of sorts together. I had never recovered from losing the mansion in Charleston. I used to tell people that one day I was going to have another historic house of my own, but I'm sure nobody believed me.

I wrote a biography of Rosalynn Carter but by the time it was published, President Carter was becoming unpopular and it made little money. John-Paul was in and out of mental hospitals every few months. He would walk into strangers' houses, say that he owned them, and get himself arrested. The police would throw him into the local jail, which Natasha had to pass on her way to school. He went through periods of great violence, threatening our lives when voices that only he could hear told him to hurt us. Once he locked us in a room; for the next half hour we knew how the hostages must have felt in Iran.

Then one day, just before Christmas of 1981, I was walking with Natasha and John Stevenson, a good friend, just across the river from Catskill in the small city of Hudson, New York. Suddenly we came upon an old red brick Federal mansion built long ago by a whaling captain. There were carved acanthus leaves over the doorway, just as there had been over the one in Charleston. "That's my house," I said.

The advance from Mother's biography enabled me to buy it, and a great healing has taken place in my heart. There we live with Vita, our water spaniel, Lady Marjorie, a Burmese cat from Scotland, and Princess Margaret, a three-legged retired German shepherd police dog rescued in New York and given to Natasha by columnist Liz Smith.

John-Paul isn't with us anymore. After sixteen trips to mental hospitals, he opened our front door to two lady Jeho-

vah's Witnesses, clad only in his birthday suit. As eleven-year-old Natasha said: "Mama, that is the last straw."
We were divorced in 1982.

Dawn Langley Simmons
Rutherford House
Hudson, New York

Michael Noakes's portrait of Dame Margaret Rutherford. (*National Portrait Gallery, London.*)

· Prologue ·

T HE tramp walked slowly along the pavement of Berke-
ley Place, Wimbledon. His clothes were old-fashioned
and threadbare; his eyes, bloodshot and vacant. His beard
was unkempt and he badly needed a haircut. In his reddened
hand was a crumpled piece of paper. The old man stopped at
Number Four, an unpretentious but very proper red brick
villa. Glancing quickly at the paper, he walked up to the front
door and hesitantly rattled the polished brass knocker.

The girl behind the starched lace cutains had seen him
coming up the street. She was thirteen years old and rather
plain. Fascinated, like the audience for a play, she watched
unseen as the old tramp paused before coming to the door. It
was as if she had always expected him; when the sound of his
knocking echoed through the small house, her young heart
was pounding.

"Who is it?" Aunt Bessie called from upstairs where she
was busy at her desk writing a letter.

1

"I don't know."

Then the girl with the green eyes slowly opened the door, managing to muster a polite smile for the elderly stranger. Neither said a word; they just stood there in the late afternoon sunlight as if taking stock of each other.

It was the old man who spoke first and the girl was surprised, for by the sound of his voice he was an educated man.

"I have brought a message from your father."

"My father." The teenager looked puzzled. "My father is dead. He died in India nursing the sick when I was a baby."

The stranger slowly shook his head and for a fleeting moment she saw the glint of madness in his tired eyes.

"Your father is alive. He sends you his love."

She was shaking now and the words were hard to get out. "I do not understand."

"Your father's shut up in Broadmoor."

Then the stranger, whom in later years she would call *King Lear,* shook his matted white mane and laughed hysterically. A moment later he was gone.

"Peggy, why are you standing there? What is the matter?"

Aunt Bessie, a small, upright, wasp-waisted figure of uncertain years, with a gold watch pinned to her formidable bosom, had reached the foot of the stairs.

"Where is Broadmoor?"

Aunt Bessie froze; it was as if she had been turned to marble.

"Broadmoor is the Asylum for the Criminally Insane."

The words came softly and reluctantly as Aunt Bessie forced herself back to reality. She cradled the now-weeping child protectively in her arms.

"My father is not dead. Oh, why did Uncle Benn and you both tell me that he was?"

Aunt Bessie was sobbing now, too. "His is a living death."

Prologue

Margaret Rutherford, known in the family as Peggy, would remember those words to the end of her days. For the rest of her life she would also be plagued with the fear that her own mind would suddenly snap, as her unfortunate father's had. In times of acute stress or overwork she would suffer from a form of melancholia that necessitated periods of complete rest, sometimes in a nursing home.

·1·
The Orphan

J UDGING by contemporary accounts, the Reverend Julius Benn was a saint. A dedicated evangelist whose conscience had been stirred by the appalling poverty and degradation found in London's East End, he had forsaken the established Church of England to become a Nonconformist. For some fifteen years he had labored at the Old Gravel Lane Meeting House, St. George-in-the-East, where at times he was ably assisted by a son, William Rutherford Benn, an aspiring silk merchant.

The father had impoverished himself working among the poor, while his son was described as being "notably generous to the needy." Aesthetic in manner and inspired by the then-popular Pre-Raphaelite art movement, William wrote poems and prose for his own amusement.

Charles Dickens gleaned authentic descriptions of opium dens and squalid tenements from Julius and William Benn, who had ministered spiritually and practically in both.

4

The Orphan

The Reverend Julius Benn was hardly of a retiring nature. He never walked when he could run, charging into the infamous opium establishments, scattering pipes and sinners in all directions. Remembering his Master's admonition to give worldly goods to the poor, the Reverend Benn was at times so financially embarrassed that family members and admiring friends took up discreet collections on his behalf. Sympathetic to juvenile delinquents, he was a leading campaigner for reform schools for them so that they should not be exposed to the horrendous Victorian prison system. When the first of these was opened, the Reverend Benn was placed in charge of it. His sense of social justice would be passed on to several of his descendants, notably Tony Benn.

On December 16, 1882, William Rutherford Benn, then twenty-seven years old, was married at All Saints, Wandsworth, to Florence Nicholson, twenty-four, a member of a scholarly middle-class family. The bridesmaid and one of the witnesses was Bessie Nicholson, older sister and a second mother to the bride. Florence and Bessie's parents were dead; another sister had committed suicide by drowning.

From all appearances, William Rutherford Benn and Florence Nicholson were made for each other; they were both born romantics. Spoiled and catered to by the practical Bessie, who knew only too well her remaining sister's precarious mental balance, Florence had fallen in love more with William's poetry than with him.

Like a doomed Brontë heroine, Florence was quite unfitted to the passionate side of marriage. William's medical report suggests that it was this initial failure to consummate their union that was responsible for his first nervous breakdown. He would fall into fits of deep depression, which alternated with bouts of "unusual excitement and irritability." On the advice of the family doctor, William was placed in the Bethnal House Asylum in East London, close enough for his concerned father to keep a kindly eye upon his condition.

Florence, a small sad-faced creature, almost boyish in appearance, returned to the sanctuary of Bessie's home in Wimbledon. Bewildered by all that had happened, she spent long hours poring over her unfortunate bridegroom's verses and making those vellum-bound albums of pressed seaweeds and wildflowers for which Victorian ladies were famous.

William's stay in the asylum proved to be short; after a few weeks the doctors thought he was ready to leave. They tactfully suggested that at least for the time being Florence and he should live apart, an arrangement to which Bessie and the Benns readily agreed. The Reverend Benn explained to his anxious daughter-in-law just how expedient it was that William should stay quietly in the country. It had been recommended that he stay at a home in the vicinty of Matlock in Derbyshire, where the man of the family would act as his "keeper," then a common arrangement for young gentlemen with problems of the mind.

Prompted by Bessie, Florence readily agreed that this further separation was in William's best interest. Besides, she had read that Matlock was one of the most beautiful spots in the whole of England. "A Gothic paradise," she told a relieved Bessie, "dripping with fantasy."

There William could take long health-giving walks, a trait one day he would pass on to their only child, and find inspiration for his verses. The Reverend Julius and Bessie, as if dealing with two adolescent children, even promised that in time Florence might be allowed to join him. Thus, William and his devoted father, fresh from nursing a house full of cholera victims, left London for the county of Derbyshire.

They arrived at Matlock Bridge February 27, 1883, engaging a sitting room and two bedrooms (the son could still hear "heavenly voices" with whom he communicated half the night, while the elderly father was in need of his sleep) in a Chesterfield Road boardinghouse close to the railroad station, owned by "a Godly and properly Christian couple," Mr. and Mrs. George Marchant.

Their new landlady noted that father and son appeared "most devoted . . . cheerful and comfortable . . . a very Jacob and Joseph." She felt honored to have such a dedicated servant of God staying in her establishment. She even placed her late grandmother's cherished blue Staffordshire chamberpot under his bed, an honor that she did not bestow upon "ordinary mortals."

More down to earth, Marchant himself was to remember that there was "nothing uncommon in the conduct of either gentleman." Because of his visitors' religious backgrounds, he seems to have made allowances for William's talking to himself and quoting liberally from the Bible.

On Saturday evening, March 4, both Benns retired early after an enjoyable day viewing the scenic attractions of the neighborhood. After an ample supper of hot steak and kidney pie, followed by a treacle and suet pudding, which Mrs. Marchant said "would keep out the cold," William had spent half an hour writing a letter to Florence. He enclosed a poem he had written describing a waterfall "hanging with icicles."

Then he kissed his father goodnight and, whistling his favorite hymn, went up to bed.

Next morning the Marchants were up early preparing breakfast for their guests, quite oblivious that anything was amiss; they did hear "a slight rapping noise at about 7 o'clock," but disregarded it. When the Benns did not come down for breakfast, their hosts were not unduly alarmed; people on holiday often liked to sleep late.

After lighting a fire in the parlor grate, George Marchant went to church, leaving his wife at home. When the father and son still failed to make an appearance, Mrs. Marchant became worried. There was no response to her knocking so she gently turned the knob of the Reverend Benn's bedroom door. It was locked, but she did hear "a peculiar noise something like snoring."

Finally, at one P.M., her husband returned from church. In response to his wife's pleading, he went upstairs and shouted for the Benns to open the door. There was only one common outer door that opened onto the landing passage; William's bedroom communicated with his father's. Slowly the door was unbolted and Marchant entered the room where, according to the *Derbyshire Times* of March 7, stood William Rutherford Benn "silent and erect in front of him in his night dress, his throat, beard, hands, night dress, legs and feet, dripping with blood, and without uttering a sound he dramatically pointed to the bed."

There lay the Reverend Julius Benn, dead, with his brains scattered over the rug. William had smashed in his father's skull with the Staffordshire chamberpot!

It was not until the arrival of the police that it was discovered William had tried to take his own life by cutting his throat with a small tortoiseshell pocket knife. Under the sensational headline MURDER AT MATLOCK, the *Derbyshire Times* further informed its readers that "the wound in his throat which appears to have been self inflicted, is not serious and doctors stated there was no danger of fatal consequences."

William's devoted brother John, who in 1892 would become the Liberal Member of Parliament for Tower Hamlets and who would name his own son William, hurried to Matlock for the two-day-long inquest. Florence, her own state of mind already frail, had collapsed upon hearing the awful news, and although Bessie wanted to accompany John Benn, she thought it best to stay home and comfort her sister.

With his sensible and compassionate view of mental sickness, John seems to have been a most enlightened man for his time. He also sought to protect the family honor, to say nothing of his own political career. During the inquest he asked the presiding coroner if his father's personal papers could be read into evidence, including the certificate from Bethnal House Asylum authorizing William's removal "for a period of rest in the country." John sought a jury's rider that would establish "the sanity or otherwise" of his unfortunate brother. The *Derbyshire Times* reported:

> Mr. Benn repeated that he thought it only fair that before the enquiry terminated, the jury should have evidence as to the son's state of mind—which would in a sense give a reason for the commission of the deed. Unless the evidence was received the facts went out to the world as being a case in which the son had murdered his father without any qualifying circumstances—it was clearly a case of lunacy.

However, the coroner was not to be swayed by John Benn's brotherly request, ruling that the jury had to confine itself to establishing how, when, and where the deceased came to his death, and that no rider could be added. The unanimous verdict was "that the deceased, Julius Benn, was wilfully murdered by his son, William Rutherford Benn."

William, "weeping like a frightened child," was then committed to the mercy of the Derbyshire Assizes on the capital charge of murder, where if found guilty he could be sentenced to death by hanging.

Taken first to the Derby Infirmary to recover from his throat wound, he was guarded around the clock. There, on Wednesday, March 14, William again attempted suicide. Choosing a time when his police guard was pulling on his heavy boots to go off duty, he leapt through a window to the ground some twenty-one feet below. Again his injuries were only minor; he hurt his back a little and sprained his right ankle.

In the meantime it had been John's sad duty to accompany his father's body, "in a coffin lined appropriately with lead as his was a *bad* corpse," home for burial. Florence did not attend the last rites but was represented by Bessie carrying "a floral tribute in good taste bearing the inscription in Florence's own bird-like handwriting: A LAST TOKEN OF RESPECT FROM WILLIAM AND FLORENCE. RESURGUM."

Following the second suicide attempt, William's mental condition further deteriorated; when on March 27 he appeared before the Honorable W. M. Jervis at the Chief Constable's office in Derby, "he was quite incoherent, calling the magistrate Pontius Pilate." He was remanded to a further appearance in early April, but because of his mental condition was unable to appear.

On April 11 William Rutherford Benn was removed to the criminal asylum at Broadmoor when an official statement reported: "It is believed a strict medical examination has been made by the doctors, who have come to the conclusion that he will never recover his sanity. The Home Secretary having ordered his removal, the case against him has been abandoned."

As is often the case with diseases of the mind, the doctors were wrong, if only temporarily. After seven years of incarceration in the dreaded Broadmoor, William was discharged to the care of his brother John.

Florence had remained devoted as ever, writing once every weekday and twice on Sunday. Because of the publicity that had surrounded the murder, William changed his surname by deedpoll to Rutherford which had been his mother's maiden name. Leaving Bessie behind to pursue her serious studies of the occult, Mr. and Mrs. Rutherford now took up residence in Balham.

Their marital relations had obviously improved, for there at 15 Dornton Road on May 11, 1892, with the indomitable Bessie acting as midwife, Florence gave birth to a daughter. They named her Margaret Taylor Rutherford.

In 1897 William and Florence Rutherford and baby Margaret left England to make a new life in far away India. There William with his good family connections was able to continue his interrupted occupation as a silk merchant. Appalled by the slums that he found in Madras and Delhi, just as his ill-fated father had been in the East End of London, William now spent long hours ministering to their sick and poor. As Florence proudly wrote home to Bessie: "William is making an earnest effort to redeem himself."

William himself often spoke of being a penitent, a fact confirmed by his brother John's grandson, Anthony Wedgwood Benn, British Member of Parliament, in a letter written me from the House of Commons on August 27, 1982: "You are right about William in India. Father [Lord Stangate] spoke of it."

The overtaxed medical authorities were only too grateful for his practical help, particularly in nursing the victims of cholera. That his efforts were not confined to the native population is attested to by an extract from a letter written by C. H. Gilpin, a young Englishman from Castor, to Margaret: "Many years ago I, as a very young man, stayed with him [William Rutherford] in Delhi. Later he nursed me through an attack of fever in Madras."

The Rutherfords' domestic life appears to have been very happy during their first months in India, for in spite of the tragedy that had blighted their marriage, they were still very much in love. They also doted upon their daughter, giving her a small white pony for her sixth birthday. As an old lady she would ask, "I wonder what became of my pony?"

The parents were overjoyed by the news that Florence was again pregnant and William considerately wondered if she should not return to England to await the birth. Florence adamantly refused but as the time for her delivery drew near, she became increasingly restless and disturbed.

With his own sorry record of mental breakdowns, William, more than anybody, understood the ominous signs. He wired for Bessie, who, brave soul that she was, made hurried preparations for the long sea journey. Her bags were already packed when another cable arrived with the shocking news that Florence was dead. It was not until nearly three months later that an almost incoherent William Rutherford, holding little Margaret by the hand, banged on Bessie's front door. Weeping, he blurted forth the cause of Florence's death. A servant had found her at dawn one morning hanging from a tree, dead.

William was never the same again. Breakdown followed breakdown, and with the exception of a few happy days spent with his friend young Gilpin in Paris, William retreated into his own world of dreams and fantasies. Today his malady would be termed a form of schizophrenia (an umbrella term covering a wide range of symptoms suffered by people who have lost touch with reality) and with modern drugs could probably have been controlled.

In October of 1902, William was admitted to the Northumberland House Asylum and when, in January 1904, he again showed homicidal tendencies, he was sent back to Broadmoor.

Hastily Bessie conferred with the ever-loyal Benn family. It was thought to be in the child Margaret's best interests that she be told her father had died. Once when she asked, as bright children do, where he was buried, Aunt Bessie was even prepared with an answer: "In the Benn family vault."

That way she did not have to invent a grave site to satisfy the curious child.

For some reason, the murder committed years before by her father had been forgotten. To protect the Benns from the stigma of admitting that a member of the family had been both mad and a murderer, Mother Rutherford was still claiming, as late as 1971, "They were like young lovers, so happy in each other's company until my mother died. My father died in tragic circumstances soon after my mother, and so I became an orphan."

Actually William stayed in Broadmoor until 1921. Then, in frail health, he was taken at the urging of his daughter— aided by her powerful Benn relations—to the City of London Asylum at Stone, near Dartford, Kent. After suffering two strokes he became quite incapacitated, and had to be wheeled onto the grounds in a flat wicker invalid carriage. There on warm, sunny days his sad green eyes "cried out for release." Mercifully he contracted pneumonia, dying August 4, 1921. He was sixty-six.

·2·
The Adopted Daughter

WITH the Benn family's approval, Margaret called Aunt Bessie "Mother." The Benns retained a lively interest in the child, though it was not always easy; she so resembled her father in looks that at times it was painful for them. They never forgot her on birthdays, Easter, and Christmas. One Easter they gave her a Fabergé egg in which throughout her life she kept a few postage stamps.

Said Margaret: "I was a grave child. My face was oval like a bantam egg and I had green eyes round as pennies. My hair was auburn-tinged and fine as floss and I wrinkled my nose like a rabbit. I was to grow into a complicated romantic like my father."

Aunt Bessie, whose maternal love already extended to her three spoiled tabby cats, Napoleon Bonaparte, Dante, and Beatrice, to say nothing of a noisy French canary named Sidney who had been smuggled into the country via Dieppe, easily took real mother love in stride. She even gave up

14

wearing Aunt Fan's big gold brooch because Margaret had complained that at kissing-time, it pricked her; she substituted a gold watch that hung from a small gold bow pinned neatly at her breast.

Although outwardly conventional in her brown serge dress and high button-up boots, Aunt Bessie was quite emancipated for a voteless spinster. As Margaret recalled: "I was allowed my own dream world, which my adoptive mother punctuated with her discipline. For instance, my back was weak, so every day I was made to lie motionless on the floor while she read to me in French. Later in my career I have been many times complimented on my carriage, ability to wear period clothes, and my meticulous French accent. This is all due to those morning sessions on the floor with Aunt Bessie."

Even so, with no other children in the house, Margaret was lonely, so Aunt Bessie encouraged her to live in her own world of make-believe—a fortunate choice for the future actress.

Margaret learned early to believe in miracles, of which she always considered her adoptive mother to be the first. "As a child I was highly emotional," she says. "If I heard a band in the street, it made me cry. I loved gay music and when the trumpets boomed and the cymbals clashed, I used to pick up my lace-edged petticoats and in my little button boots dance with abandoned joy."

Early in life Aunt Bessie introduced Margaret to her own personal belief in psychic phenomena: that nobody ever really died in the spiritual sense. Aunt Bessie fervently believed that loved ones who had passed on were always at hand in times of trouble.

Said Margaret, "Aunt Bessie believed herself to be gifted with psychic powers. She was quite sure that if one asked a dead relative to intercede personally with God for something sensible like a new pair of Sunday shoes—of course in a nice, ladylike way—there was a good chance that the prayer would be granted."

During the school holidays Margaret's cousin, Graham Nicholson, who she said, "was like a brother to me," would visit.These were red-letter days for the lonely little girl; the two children would sit side by side at Aunt Bessie's enormous red mahogany desk, which had been her father's, and write their own little plays. "Graham always started off well but never finished his," complained Margaret, who even then was very serious about her work. "But I lived every moment of my plays, for the characters were real as life to me."

Margaret and Aunt Bessie were always invited to the home of Graham's parents for Christmas Day. Margaret's beautifully hand-smocked party frock, an annual Christmas gift from her wealthy Benn relatives to "the little orphan-no-longer," was much admired. She still did not have an inkling that her unfortunate father was alive and spending a loveless holiday season in a lunatic asylum.

As was the fashion in those time of self-entertainment, family theatricals, especially melodrama, were enacted. (Surprisingly Aunt Bessie's favorite was *Maria Martin,* or *The Murder in the Red Barn.*) On such play-giving occasions, Margaret and Graham, who were very compatible, "had to endure our cousin Muriel, who was so anti-theater that I had to write a part for her where she was confined to a dark dreary cupboard for most of the performance."

At the age of eight, Margaret was to have played *The Bad Fairy* in the Nicholsons' annual Christmas play; when Graham conveniently "went down with an ear infection and the mumps," she obligingly took over his Fairy Prince role as well.

She never forgot that first all-important entrance, as one of the adults labored behind the scenes to produce necessary claps of thunder from a rolling pin and a battered tin tray! A professional actress in the friendly audience gave her her first good notice, as the Bad Fairy. "The child has great histrionic power," she announced to a proud Aunt Bessie. "One has to be really good to be bad."

That night Margaret Rutherford went to bed filled with dreams of growing up to be a great actress.

At Wimbledon High School Peggy, as Margaret was known to her schoolmates, was editor of *The Pinc,* their own newspaper. The title was made up of the initials of Peggy, Irene, Nellie, and Clarissa, all fellow students. (Nellie was the sister of Robert Graves, the poet.)

Then Aunt Bessie decided to make what Margaret called "the Supreme Sacrifice." Deciding that it was time that her beloved child "be prepared for the real world . . . for she simply cannot live in her own little fairyland for ever," Aunt Bessie enrolled her at Raven's Croft School in Upper Warlingham, Surrey. (It moved from Upper Warlingham to the bracing seaside town of Seaford, Sussex, in September of 1909.)

When Margaret first went to Raven's Croft, she was fourteen years old; the year was 1906. She had only learned the terrible secret concerning the family murder, and that her father was still alive, the year before. It was little wonder that she had "gone into a fit of deep depression with long periods of silence broken occasionally by crying." A completely new environment seemed the most sensible solution for the unhappy child.

Raven's Croft was a reputable school for girls, founded by two exceptional sisters, Margaret and Isabelle Mullins. When Miss Isabelle asked Margaret what she would like to be when she grew up, she received the matter-of-fact reply: "As I am already a lady, I want nothing better than to be a professional actress." The little gold pince-nez spectacles dropped off Miss Isabelle's nose. She was shocked at such a revelation. "I suspect," said Margaret, "that the poor dear had visions of Lily Langtry the actress and her unhealthy liaison with King Edward the Seventh."

Next day Margaret was confronted by both headmistresses, who proclaimed it their joint opinion that "young ladies did not become actresses, professional or otherwise." Instead, as her piano playing showed much promise, they decided that for the next six years Margaret Rutherford should study for the associate examination of the Royal Academy of Music, which in due course she would pass with honors. Years later, after the school had moved further along the coast to Eastbourne, her name, *P. Rutherford,* remained painted on one of the prefect boards that hung in the schools's assembly hall.

Margaret confessed to being "nearly always late for everything" at Raven's Croft. Throughout her subsequent life as an adult, unless it affected her work as an actress, time never concerned her.

She tried hard to overcome her dislike of sports, thinking herself as being "both sensational and at the same time a martyr" after scoring four runs in a girls' cricket match! Cricket and hockey were not played after the move to Seaford, where instead Raven's Croft became one of the first British schools to take up the game of lacrosse.

Mother did not think much of blood sports, either. When my expensive mink coat was stolen in Charleston, South Carolina, in 1970, she penned me a note of consolation: "I never did care for you attired in those unfortunate little skins."

One year while at Seaford, Margaret played Prospero in Shakespeare's *The Tempest,* which was performed by "the big girls." Her schoolfriend Dorothy Whatmore (later Dame Dorothy Vaisey) recalled years later that "Peggy Rutherford was a great favorite of the younger girls, in whom she took a special motherly interest." The longing for children of her own was always strong, even then. She stayed on at school an extra year, "because," she said, "I wanted to take care of the little ones." As she told Gwen Robyns, the noted biographer, and close friend of the late Princess Grace of Monaco, "I have always had this motherly instinct, and people find it easy to share their problems with me."

Nineteen hundred and eleven. Margaret's schooldays were over at last and she returned to her home in Wimbledon. There she became a familiar figure on her bicycle, with leather music case swinging from the handlebars. To the world she seemed a happy soul, singing or reciting poetry aloud as she rode to her piano students' homes.

"To me, unfortunately, being a music teacher was only a way to make a living and help my adoptive mother, now noticeably older and slower of step. I was not a good music teacher. My thoughts were always far away with an unseen audience.

"Besides, I was often far too honest in telling the parents, when their unfortunate offspring hated music, that no power in the world could ever make it like playing the piano.

"Once I overheard a pretty little boy named Albert Edward exclaim: 'Here comes that nasty Miss Rutherford to give me my old piano lesson.' It hurt me very much."

She was still determined to be an actress.

On Sunday afternoons, if the weather was fine, Margaret always pushed Aunt Bessie through the familiar streets in her wicker bathchair, which the latter steered with the aid of a sticklike device in the front. Margaret and the large bathchair dwarfed the regal little lady wearing the big hat overly decorated with whatever flowers were in season . . . and always holly at Christmas.

"I have always had a distaste for artificial flowers," Margaret would one day comment, "and now they have seen fit to invent ones fashioned out of plastic."

Sometimes when they were walking through the cemetery Margaret would get carried away with the Shakespearean character she was invisibly playing and "break into a nice little trot."

"Careful, child," Aunt Bessie would caution, "or we shall run into Cousin Ethel's cross."

The two women were far from well-off, for the years at Raven's Croft had been a serious drain on Aunt Bessie's finances. Neither would have dreamed of telling either the Benn or the Nicholson family of their plight, while borrowing money was demeaning and out of the question. Besides, there was still the silver teapot and their jewelry heirlooms that could be sold! If her child needed private lessons in order to become an actress, then these she should have. Cousin William Benn (John Benn's son and that other unfortunate William's namesake) recommended that Margaret take lessons from Acton Bond, an old Shakespearean actor.

"William says that Mr. Acton has impeccable manners and has assured me that he will not make unseemly advances towards her," Aunt Bessie confided to her diary.

As a result of these lessons, Margaret Rutherford obtained a certificate of proficiency in elocution. Speeding through the streets on her bicycle en route to a waiting pupil, she practiced "pure, loud Es and rounded Os."

During the sad years of World War I she returned to her first great love, poetry, reciting to groups of soldiers home on leave from the front, and to the injured in hospitals.

Meanwhile, she acted with the local dramatic society, "never refusing a role, however humble, that was offered me," and continued to teach music. "I might just as well have taken on a paper route," she lamented.

After the war Margaret's situation only worsened. Aunt Bessie suffered a series of strokes, but to the end her mind was strangely clear at intervals. With her usual sense of order she calmly announced one morning to a tearful Margaret, "It is quite unfair to you. I am taking much too long to die." Moments later she was gone.

·3·
The Would-Be Actress

"I BEGAN my stage career late in life and the beginning was not easy. If you want to be an actor or an actress passionately enough, you will be—but it is up to you to persevere, despite all obstacles."

Margaret was now thirty-three years old, an age when the most she could look forward to was life as an old maid with a cat. The year was 1925; she was really alone for the first time. With her adoptive mother, Aunt Bessie, to care for, any thoughts of marriage had been out of the question. Besides, she had never met any man who had sparked even a remote romantic interest.

With that determination inherent to her nature, she took Aunt Bessie's small legacy of seven hundred fifty pounds and put the Wimbledon house on the market. Then, having left "the arpeggios and Wimbledon Common behind me," Margaret promptly rented a room next door to London's notorious Holloway Prison, where even her new landlord told her:

"Young ladies like you don't usually want to rent a room on this street."

> The death of my adoptive mother was the first tragedy to really affect me. She was all things in one: mother, aunt and best friend. However, I remembered the old saying: "Told of a death; hear of a birth." Cousin William's thoughtful wife has given birth to a little boy yesterday morning (April 3). Thank God, he didn't arrive on April Fool's Day. He is destined to go through life as Anthony Neil Wedgwood Benn but I quite expect we will all call him Tony.

Only my mother would have advertised for a maid to take care of a single room. Then again, only Mother would engage a maid well into her sixties, who as part of her own recommendation said she had second sight!

"I am very bad with a sewing needle," Margaret was always the first to confess. Housekeeping was not her forte either. Devon-born Elizabeth Orphin took one look at the chaos in Margaret's bed-sitter and exclaimed in her West Country accent: "Missy, I will be a second mother to you," and for the next eight years she was.

"Although she communicated with the dead over breakfast, Elizabeth saw that nothing was wasted and we had nourishing soups, stew, cream puffs, and treacle puddings. She did all the mending and cleaning and completely took charge."

Remembering those days, Mother told me: "I wrinkled my nose like a determined rabbit and never turned back again."

Dorothy Whatmore, Margaret's former schoolmate, had written her a letter of introduction to John Drinkwater, poet and dramatist. Drinkwater in turn referred her to Robert Atkins, a former head of the Old Vic School. Atkins thought she should see Andrew Leigh, who had succeeded him in that formidable position.

As a result, the would-be actress received a letter saying she had been granted an audition with Lilian Baylis, then affectionately (or otherwise) known as the "Queen of the Old Vic." Such stage and screen greats as John Gielgud, Laurence Olivier, Edith Evans, and Ralph Richardson were all to owe Miss Baylis a debt for their early training.

Margaret was elated. Wearing her best green dress (green was her favorite color) and a pair of fashionable new Gloria Swanson pointed shoes that looked somewhat out of place on her rather large, broad feet, she jumped on the bus for Waterloo. At long last, she hoped, her chance had come.

Miss Baylis was a no-nonsense lady and, to Margaret that day, quite a frightening one. With thick-lensed glasses, mousey hair, and what Margaret described as "a one-sided smile." she was flanked on either side by a snippy terrier.

Margaret Rutherford's audition was a near disaster. "My new shoes let out miaowing squeaks every time I walked, even making the dogs bark."

At the end of the audition the Queen of the Old Vic pronounced, in her most gloomy, godlike voice: "Dear girl, I think production might be a safer line than acting."

A somewhat dejected Margaret and "those horrible Gloria Swanson shoes" made their way home to Holloway, where "gentle Elizabeth tried to cheer me up with a good cup of tea and a plum-heavy."

A few mornings later, when Margaret felt "strangely close to dear Aunt Bessie," Elizabeth came charging in with the morning mail. Margaret Rutherford had been accepted as a trainee actress for the September 1925–May 1926 season.

"Well," sniffed Elizabeth as if sharing a secret with the Great Beyond, "your Aunt Bessie knew it all along."

Although my mother is best remembered as a sort of feminine version of Winston Churchill, never admitting defeat, she lived in much awe of Miss Baylis during her days at the Old Vic School.

Lilian Baylis liked to sit in her office, feet up on a chair, listening to classical music played on her crystal radio set; only the dogs were allowed to disturb her.

Margaret discovered the Old Vic to be "a just but hard school." There the students were obliged to take any role given them; on December 21, 1925, she received what she called "a wonderful Christmas gift . . . my first speaking role." She played The Fairy with the Long Nose in *Harlequin Jack Horner and the Enchanted Pie.* She wore her papier-mâché snout with distinction.

The second offering of the evening was a nativity play, *The Child in Flanders* by Cicely Hamilton, with Edith Evans playing a mute Angel Gabriel. Gabriel's lines were spoken off-stage by Margaret, who was obliged to remove her extra nose as she dashed to the rear. Wrote an outspoken critic: "Edith Evans' elocution has greatly improved."

After winning a student competition, Margaret played Lady Capulet to Edith Evans' Nurse in *Romeo and Juliet.* Esmond Knight, Frank Vosper, and Baliol Holloway were in the same cast; all five were destined for successful careers in the theater.

In *Caesar and Cleopatra,* Margaret had one line to recite over Caesar's bier. "I enunciated each word so that a deaf man in the upper circle could hear it."

"I was grateful to be doing at last what I loved most," she said. But, after giving her eleven roles to play in nine months, Miss Baylis casually called Margaret into her office, turned off the crystal radio, and told the dogs to be quiet. Then the Queen of the Old Vic with regal finality announced that she was sorry but there would be no room for Margaret the next season.

"Somehow you just do not fit in!"

In fairness to Lilian Baylis, some years later when Margaret Rutherford had her first West End success, in *Spring Meeting,* the Queen of the Old Vic sent her former subject a letter of congratulations, saying how wrong she had been to let her go.

Many would have been crushed but not my mother. With her rented Holloway room and Elizabeth to support, she had no time for tears. Out came the bicycle and the music sheets, and for two miserable years that seemed to last forever she again taught piano in Wimbledon. Yet there was no doubt in her mind that one day she would be recognized as a professional actress.

"Looking back," she said, "those months were not wasted. There must have been a meaning in it all, but at the time my heart ached."

Instead of dwelling on the Old Vic's rejection, she quickly joined the Wimbledon Amateur Theatrical Society where she first displayed that natural gift she had for bringing laughter to her audience. This was in an army dishwashing scene, where she managed to break more cups than she wiped.

"It was then," she said, "that I felt the joy it gave me in being able to make people laugh and forget themselves. . . . Never look down on the humble art of washing-up. Who knows but in every shining cup and saucer will be reflected a character from your next play."

She also found a stage godmother in actress Ethel Royale, who had successfully appeared opposite Cedric Hardwicke in *The Farmer's Wife.*

As a special favor, Margaret's uncle, Guy Nicholson, asked Miss Royale, a personal friend, to see his niece in the Wimbledon production of *Hay Fever,* and to tell him truthfully if his niece should continue in her efforts to be an actress.

Margaret was playing the comic maid and knew in advance that Ethel Royale would be in the audience. "I can truthfully say that I did not feel so nervous on my wedding day."

Afterward, Miss Royale assured Uncle Guy that "your Peggy is lovable and will make people laugh, both rare qualities in the theater."

For the first time Margaret had been told by a member of the acting profession that she was a natural clown. More importantly, Ethel Royale had given her just the encouragement that she so badly needed at that period in her life.

"I was truly invigorated," said Margaret, "although I still yearned to play serious roles. I did not want to be known as *that dotty lady*."

Thanks to her stage godmother's interest, the bicycle went back into storage as, with typical Rutherford gusto, she made an all-out attack on the world of the London theater. The respectable background of the YWCA hostel would be her advance post.

"There are times, dear child," she would tell me, "that even individualists like you and I must sacrifice our principles just a little bit and conform."

Mother also maintained that she had made some of her best contacts "over the garden fence and on top of a double-decker bus." It was a girl at the hostel who gave her an introduction to Nigel Playfair, director of the Lyric Theatre in Hammersmith.

Thirty-six years old and still blissfully innocent of the ways of the world, Margaret decided to use rouge and lipstick for the first time. In addition, she bought the kind of dress she thought an actress should wear. On Joan Crawford it would have been a success, but as worn by Margaret Rutherford, it was a major disaster.

On meeting her, Playfair's face registered "absolute horror." Extremely sensitive, for often unfeeling people had laughed that "somebody with so plain a face should have the sauce to think she could ever become a leading lady," Margaret was convinced that Nigel Playfair thought her "a loose woman."

Next morning she wrote him a letter apologizing for "my unseemly appearance." Touched by its simple charm, the director, known for being able to draw the best out of people, immediately granted Margaret a second interview. This time he engaged her to understudy Mabel Terry-Lewis, Winifred Evans, and Margaret Everest in the play *A Hundred Years Old*. Miss Terry-Lewis obligingly became ill one night, allowing Margaret to take her place as Doña Filomena, complete with a black lace Spanish mantilla.

Margaret was very nervous until she was told that her favorite cousin, that same little boy who had so conveniently come down with the mumps when they were children, and who was now the scholarly Professor Nicholson, was in the audience. "Then," said she, "a magical calm came over me, for I knew that Aunt Bessie, my second mother, button-up boots and all, was at my side."

After working steadily for fifteen weeks, during which time she was gaining confidence and experience, Margaret was unemployed until April of 1929 while the faithful Elizabeth "did her best to fatten me up on her nourishing stews, for I was painfully thin." Actually, when she was not working, Margaret suffered from fits of depression, a forewarning of things to come. At times she was overwhelmed by the fear that she might one day go mad like her unfortunate father. She was more than relieved when a kindly neighbor told her that Fulham's Grand Theatre was searching for a mature-looking actress to play Madame Vinard in an adaptation of George du Maurier's novel *Trilby*. Margaret got the part; the season opened on April 21 under the direction of Robert W.

Fenn and Gerard Neville. The Grand was a happy, family-type theater where a box for four cost only ten shillings and sixpence. To sit in the gallery cost only sixpence!

From April to December 1929, Margaret appeared in twenty-seven different roles, ranging from La Vengeance in Dickens' *A Tale of Two Cities* ("I still shudder when I think of having to knit next to that guillotine") to Aggie in Gilbert Emery's *Tarnish,* to which, the theater management advised, "we only invite adults, for it depicts the realities of life."

Waking at dawn, she regularly clutched a hot-water bottle as she learned her lines while still in bed. The great variety of roles that she played gave Margaret Rutherford a lasting respect for repertory, calling it "the university of the acting profession." Her only complaint was that she could find little time for speech study and breath control practice. She did learn what she calls "the rudiments of stage makeup, which has always fascinated me" when, dressed in a brightly colored robe, she played Chi Li in *The Green Beetle.* She found the art of changing her face into that of a Chinese woman "fraught with difficulties. . . . I eventually managed to look convincing." In those days she was still minus all those splendid double chins that were to become her trademark and fortune.

In October 1930 Margaret was "an interesting" Mrs. Coade in J. M. Barrie's *Dear Brutus,* then playing at the Epsom Little Theatre in Surrey. Margaret Rawlings was also in the cast. However Margaret Rutherford's stay in pleasant Epson ended when a telegram arrived from the Oxford Playhouse offering her a meaty role in the Ben Travers comedy hit, *Thark.*

The Oxford Repertory enjoyed an excellent reputation, which she knew would help in getting better roles. Reluctantly she said goodbye to Margaret Rawlings, whose work she "particularly admired."

Before going on to Oxford she dropped by London's Aldwych Theatre to borrow the costumes that Mary Brough had worn in the original West End production of *Thark*. These were carefully packed in Aunt Bessie's domed trunk, together with a ready-made false bosom—further evidence of how really slim she was in those days. The eternal innocent, she called them "my Salomes."

She later declared that God Almighty, Cupid, and Aunt Bessie (in that order) were responsible for getting her the role at Oxford. Just as she arrived by taxi at the theater, out rushed the most handsome young man she had ever seen. So intent was he on getting to a local Armistice memorial service that he did not even notice her. His name was Stringer Davis.

Great romantic that she was, Mother always insisted it to be "love at first sight."

"There was that special something about Mr. Davis. He just *had* to be an actor, and of course, believe in ghosts!"

Margaret spent her first evening in Oxford watching Stringer play a World War I soldier in the drama *Thunder in the Air*. It was a very serious role for an actor who thought himself best in light comedy. Touching on the various facets of a young lieutenant's life, it ended with his shooting himself in action.

Margaret was particulary receptive to the scene in which the soldier's ghost returns to what had been his happy childhood home. It was the kind of heaven shared with dear familiar places in which she liked to believe. In the years that followed she would tease Stringer that "you made me weep the first night that I saw you."

Mother returned to the boardinghouse where she was staying, feeling, as she said, "a strange disquiet."

"I was just like a honeybee tasting its first sip of honeysuckle."

They did exchange a few words next day at rehearsal, where, she confessed, "I must have been a sight to behold in my wildly comic costume and billowing Salomes." None of it gave her confidence in the impression she was making on Stringer Davis, seven years her junior.

But in her own eagerness to know him better, she had underestimated his powers of perception.

"To me, Margaret was always beautiful and my first impression of her was a deep one. I felt that I must somehow stop her from wearing those funny clothes. I wanted to see her in a sensitive role, for I was sure that there was a sincere, straight person underneath."

His feelings never changed; when they were both old and a famous artist painted her portrait, he complained rather testily to me: "Daughter, your mother has a pretty pink complexion. That man has given her a green one!"

During those blissful Oxford days, Margaret often found time to lunch with a close friend from Raven's Croft days, Elfrida Down, now Mrs. Kettleborough. Elfrida found Peggy, as she called her, through their mutual friend, Ruth Troward, senior music mistress at the school.

Mrs. Kettleborough, later a nurse who trained at Guy's Hospital, London, recalls: "Ruth Troward lived and stayed with me, and Peggy visited her at my little house, so we often met. I knew Peggy in a homely way that her more eminent friends may not have seen."

Margaret remained in Oxford for two other plays, where she found time to get to know Stringer better. His parents were living apart and to his credit he was loyal to both of them, a trait that Margaret admired immediately. He seemed devoted to, if somewhat under the thumb of his mother, a lady with pretensions of grandeur who clung to a large, rambling old house at Reading long after she had lost the financial means to afford it. Stringer's full name was James Buckley Stringer Davis, but Margaret soon shortened that to Tuft, because of the hair that stood up on top of his head. Mama Davis was horrified!

"I tried so hard in those early days to hide my private feelings about this man in my life," Mother once said. "I apparently failed, as everyone later told me that they were aware that I was in love with him. I know that I could not take my eyes off him. . . . If he noticed me at all, I still felt it was because he had immaculate manners and treated all the ladies in the company with gallantry."

Somewhat reluctantly she returned to Epsom for a Christmas engagement in *The Sport of Kings*. Before leaving she shyly gave Stringer a tiny package beautifully wrapped in green paper with ribbon to match. He was deeply touched when he found inside a small traveling mirror in a leather case.

Being the man he was, he reciprocated. His first gift to Margaret was an outsize Jerusalem cherry bush in a red flowerpot. It was delivered to her on stage during the curtain calls following the Boxing Day matinee "by a slightly bewildered stagehand."

Before returning to the Oxford Playhouse, Margaret took a train to Eastbourne to visit her old school, where Margaret L. Clark, then a student, recalls "the future Dame Margaret personally greeting me." Loyalty was a Rutherford trait. She never forgot a friend or somebody who had shown her a kindness.

In January 1931 Margaret returned to the Oxford Playhouse for another busy season of repertory. A photograph survives of her with a black lace mantilla as Doña Barbarita in *The Romantic Young Lady*. There is kindness and compassion in those deep-set eyes, and in the way she is holding her fan, even a touch of seductiveness.

The final offering of a successful season was Oscar Wilde's *The Importance of Being Earnest,* in which she played her first Lady Bracknell, a prophetic choice, for this particular play would prominently figure in her later career.

In April, Margaret was invited to join Esmé Church's company at Croydon's Greyhound Theatre, which had once been an old coaching house. At her suggestion, Stringer Davis was also in the cast. "He was so handsome," she said, "and all the younger actresses were infatuated with his good looks. They all wondered what he could see in me. Poor dear, he used to get understandably upset when they teased him about going out with his *mother!*"

Margaret had great respect for Esmé Church as a director. She repeatedly said later on that she owed Miss Church a great deal. At Croydon, Margaret also had the opportunity to perform with Donald Wolfit in Henrik Ibsen's *The Master Builder.* Writing me on January 4, 1982, after seeing his play *The Dresser,* said to have been based on Wolfit's life, the playwright Ronald Harwood made this interesting observation: "Alas, I never met Dame Margaret, whom I greatly admired. I do, however, remember Sir Donald Wolfit saying that she was the best Mrs. Solness he ever played with; he also said she had the qualities of a *great* tragic actress—and he did not use the word 'great' lightly."

It was while she was playing the tragic Aline Solness that C. B. Cochran, the famed producer, was in the audience searching out new talent. He watched intently as Aline attended to her plants with an affection that most women would bestow upon their children. Turning to Esmé, he demanded in the loudest of whispers, "Who is that woman? She is brilliant! Where did you find her?"

Esmé said that she was Margaret Rutherford. Cockie, as he was affectionately known, replied, "I wonder why I have never heard of her before?"

Although Cockie did not offer Margaret a role in one of

his own productions, he did spread the good word that she had "a great dramatic future." Stringer, of course, agreed, while Esmé Church saw both the great tragedienne and the great comedienne in the actress.

One day Esmé found Margaret musing in her dressing room. "Oh, Esmé," she said, her face aglow, "wouldn't it be wonderful if I could play in *Romeo and Juliet?*"

Years later while living in retirement at Banbury, Esmé Church told Margaret: "I tactfully explained, I hope, that at thirty-nine years of age you were too old for the part. It was a case of the true actor inside you burning to be released beyond the barriers of the physical. But you were insistent and answered: 'If no one will let me play Juliet, then one day I'll take out a company on my own'."

Even then, Mother was beginning to be typecast much against her will. Accepting the inevitable with grace, she acknowledged, however reluctantly: "The parts I had been given had begun to show signs of the eccentricity that I later developed into my own special technique."

By this time Margaret had increased her repertoire with the works of Ibsen, Pinero, Maugham, and Coward. That October she returned to work in another six plays, including *Mary Rose* by the popular playwright J. M. Barrie (she played Mrs. Morland), and Arnold Ridley's comedy, *The Ghost Train,* standing out as the hilarious Miss Bourne.

Said she: "I became like a squirrel hoarding and cherishing to myself each of the acting experiences these great writers had given me. I was always trying to interpret the role as the producer wished it and yet remain faithful to my own beliefs."

Her ultimate goal was the West End, yet when the Oxford season ended in December, that dream still seemed far away. But shortly afterward she was given an introduction to Tyrone Guthrie, then a dynamic young producer. (Later, after many years of association with the Old Vic, Guthrie would turn his talents westward to the Shakespeare Festival in Stratford, Ontario, and the Minnesota Repertory Theatre.)

By this time Margaret Rutherford had gained no small reputation as a character actress. Guthrie met with her to give words of encouragement, but no job. "Bombard me," he invited, and she did just that: Every achievement, however small, was duly reported to him in her own flamboyant handwriting.

Fortunately she then met Oliver Walter, who had taken over the Greater London Players from Lena Ashwell. Rex Harrison, also destined for stardom, was sometimes in the company; she particularly admired his "authority and accurate timing."

The company worked hard, doing weekly repertory in one-night stands. While playing at Dovercourt, Reading, she could see her "Tuft"; they took long walks down country lanes together. He would pick her large bunches of wildflowers, carefully explaining the correct botanical names of each with their particular gender. Then he would plait a ribbon of long grasses with which to tie them together.

Margaret and he had picnics on the river, borrowing his mother's canoe for nostalgic wanderings down the Thames. They even went sprinting together where, much to his surprise, Stringer found that his forty-year-old companion could easily outrun him.

"And I was considered rather good," he told me.

He also found she was a very good swimmer who was always game for a quick dip in the frigid river on the chilliest of English mornings.

"Of course," she recalled: "Tuft always remembered to bring a stale currant bun purchased for tuppence at the local bakery for his beloved dickey-birds."

It was while they were at Reading that Stringer was to try his hand at directing, with a play called *The Fanatics* in which Margaret was to play. There was also a personal reason for this; to show Margaret that "I had been correct all the time. That she was perfectly suitable for straight roles."

She was more jittery than usual when the cast took its places for rehearsal. "Then" she said, "Stringer joined us and suddenly everything came alive for me. We were rehearsing a scene in which I played an elderly friend of the family. I sat down by the gas fire in a bedroom surrounded by young people. They wanted to know about my first love affair. Stringer directed me gently and allowed me to tell the story with the simplicity that I felt was right for the part."

Stringer read more into the reading than even she had intended he should. There was no doubt in his heart that Margaret Rutherford was in love with him.

·4·
The Actress

I F Margaret Rutherford had a fairy godmother responsible
for getting her her first West End role, then it must have
been her old schoolfriend, Dame Dorothy Vaisey.

Dorothy's brother, Arthur Whatmore, had a fine reputation as a director in repertory. Dorothy was always remind-
ing him of her friend who was trying so hard to become an
established actress. One day he called to say he was directing
Wild Justice by James Dale at the Lyric Theatre, Hammersmith (which was known as the "Blood Tub" because of its
tradition for roaring melodramas). He wondered if Peggy
Rutherford would be interested in a "very small part."

She was duly cast as the murderer's charwoman and went
unnoticed by the critics. Quite unexpectedly she learned that
the play was being transferred to the West End's Vaudeville
Theatre.

At forty-one years old, when some women are already
grandmothers, Margaret had finally reached her goal.

It was May of 1933.

After *Wild Justice,* Margaret found herself understudying Muriel Aked and Jean Cadell in *Birthday* at the Cambridge Theatre. Then came a Sunday night performance of *The Master Builder* for the Scandinavian Society. She again played Aline Solness; Donald Wolfit directed and recreated his own original Solness role. John Clements and Beatrix Lehmann were newcomers to the cast.

"It was a part I enjoyed because of its tragic perception," Margaret said.

The Master Builder was transferred to the Embassy Theatre, Swiss Cottage, that April for the season. Margaret accepted Donald Wolfit's invitation to go with it. In 1934 the Embassy had a glowing reputation under the adventurous leadership of Ronald Adams; that very year five of its previous productions had transferred to and were playing in the West End at once.

Ivor Brown was the first critic of importance to notice Margaret Rutherford in this production of *The Master Builder,* and for the rest of her life she spoke gratefully of him.

In 1935 the theater world was talking about *Hervey House,* written by that fine American actress, Jane Cowl, under the pen-name of C. R. Avery. It seemed to have the makings of a dazzling London production, with Gertrude Lawrence and Fay Compton leading the all-star cast.

Once more Margaret wrote in her unique handwriting to director Tyrone Guthrie for a possible role. Back came his now-familiar refusal and regrets, and as if to add insult to injury, the words: "There is nothing the least like you in the play."

One Saturday, three weeks later, Margaret's telephone rang. It was Guthrie's secretary asking her to come the next day to read for the role of Lady Nancy, which had originally been intended for Athene Seyler, whose management had since refused to release her.

Recalled Margaret: "So they sent for me to come and read the part. It was Palm Sunday, the clocks had just been put on an hour, the sun was shining, the clouds were flying, and I went up to the Haymarket in all my glory."

Glorious or not, she had forgotten to put her own clock forward, arriving a full hour late for the audition. Sensing her embarrassment, Guthrie was quick to forgive her. He took her hand in his and led her onstage. There, standing in the raw glare of the spotlight, she read her part for the first time, pausing at the end, only to blurt out what she thought to be her own inadequacy.

"I wish I were more innately this woman."

There was a long pause, then Guthrie shouted: "Read it again. I think you can do it."

Again Margaret read the part and then, after what seemed to her an eternity, a young man who had been sitting next to Guthrie, Hugh Beaumont, better known in the theater world as "Binkie," announced, "There is nothing else to say except that we want you."

Eric Keown, in his book about my mother, grandly described the play as "a kind of political cavalcade that combined a notable disregard for the facts of history with a vastly sentimental respect for the British way of life, as exemplified by a famous mansion and its noble occupants." Margaret played a somewhat tragic spinster (at least *she* saw the character that way), elegantly dressed all in black with "a splendid hat adorned with a swirling osprey feather." Margaret had learned to smoke at the Old Vic "for her nerves," as well-meaning friends had told her. Now in *Hervey House* she was obliged to puff "on an expensive Cuban cigar as if I really were enjoying it."

Gertrude Lawrence was particularly kind, giving her great

encouragement at the first rehearsal. "Margaret was so sweet
. . . so eager to please; in addition to which she was quite
unaffected and blissfully innocent of life."

Molly McArthur's sets were dazzling; the fashionable
crowd adored them on opening night. In her own words,
Margaret's reviews were "remarkable; I simply could not understand why people had been so kind."

She felt embarrassed, not to mention lonely, when over-
night, she was transported from the supporting players' com-
munal dressing room to one of her very own. Unfortunately,
however, the play folded in a few weeks. Margaret felt more
sorry for Gertrude Lawrence, who was not used to failures,
than for herself.

Stringer sent a message of consolation signed simply
TUFT and tied to a rather wilted bunch of mistletoe (she
never did discover where he had found it; it wasn't even
Christmas). Elizabeth Orphin, her maid with second sight,
shrugged her shoulders upon hearing the news of the closing.
Looking up toward heaven, she declared somewhat sol-
emnly: "You will soon hear of another part."

Whether as a result of Elizabeth's prophecy or those good
first-night notices, Margaret was offered the memorable role
of Miss Flower in a new Guthrie production, Robert Morley's *Short Story.*

For the rest of her life Robert Morley would remain Margaret's devoted friend. A practical comfort when she suffered
her frightening bouts of melancholia, at the end he was destined to read her funeral oration.

As a playwright and actor he has had an interesting career.
Perhaps his most memorable portrayal was in the motion
picture *Saraband for Dead Lovers,* in which, as the mad King
George III, wearing a gorgeous dressing gown, he played the
organ at Windsor Castle. In his later years he has lightened
the hearts of many Americans as British Airways' genial am-

bassador-at-large. Waving a small Union Jack he brightens newspaper ads and with or without the flag, is heard on radio.

Short Story was not all smooth sailing for Margaret. With the help of a friend in the wardrobe department, she chose "a fantastic outfit to suit the lady's parochial soul" to play Miss Flower. Shocked by her new appearance, Tyrone Guthrie, again the director, gently told her to go and change back into her own everyday clothes.

Her skirts were too long and her dresses too bright, yet they expressed to perfection the character my mother had become.

It was during the run of *Short Story* that she was to experience her first case of professional jealousy, from, of all people, Marie Tempest, then nearing the end of a long, distinguished stage career. (She would die in 1942.)

Miss Tempest, who became a Dame in 1937, was a law unto herself. Fellow performers were expected to arrive properly dressed for morning rehearsals, and the actors were obliged to wear dinner jackets for those held in the evening.

Of *Short Story*, critic James Agate, whose pronouncements, Margaret said, were "either revered or reviled," wrote:

> The play rather resolves itself into a contention for a bone which isn't there. This being so, there is no play to run off with. But if there were it would now be in the reticule of Miss Margaret Rutherford, who as a ruthless village spinster—a Miss Flite in villeggiatura—entrances and convulses the house every moment she is on the stage. The scene in which this tigerish mouse wrestles with another caller (of all people, Rex Harrison) for the telephone, and finally secures it with a kick on the ankle, is the best thing in the play.

Miss Tempest had also seen the *Daily Mirror* critic's remark: "Margaret Rutherford made the comedy hit of the show."

Sending for Margaret, Marie Tempest imperiously told her, "I am not accustomed to having a play stolen from under my nose."

Although it was common theater knowledge that one simply did not oppose Miss Tempest, Margaret did! Quite firmly she replied: "I intend to play my part as well as I can."

Marie Tempest seemed to have forgotten that back in 1885 she had suffered her own first experience of stage jealousy, of which she later wrote:

> The star was the first unpleasant and the most cruel woman I have ever known in the theatre. I had to walk over to her in one scene and sing, while she was supposed to be sleeping. She was always hideously awake and as I sang, she would mutter foul names at me. I have always been haunted by my first sight of pathetic and malicious jealousy and I have watched for signs of it in myself with alarm.

Never one to harbor grudges against anybody, Margaret reported with obvious relief: "Later we became great friends and respected each other's techniques, and whereas in *Short Story,* Marie Tempest 'dictated laughs,' I commanded them."

Robert Morley said it even better: "Margaret can root out a laugh like a truffle hound!" He also provided the following interesting insight:

> Margaret was of course a great eccentric and, like Flora Robson, she came to the professional stage comparatively late in life. Discovered by the most brilliant and mischievous of directors, Tyrone Guthrie, he was determined that in the first play I ever wrote, *Short Story,* she should steal the play.
>
> She duly obliged, although she faced a formidable and far more experienced cast which included Marie Tempest, Sybil Thorndike, Ursula Jean, A. E. Mathews, and Rex Harrison. In a short telephone encounter with Rex she brought the house down and scooped the notices, such as

they were. She played the local village do-gooder and or-
ganiser of fetes, and bested Marie Tempest both on and off
stage.

Marie, realising and naturally enough not relishing the
threat she posed, finally summoned her to the dressing
room and attempted to subdue her tenacity and strength of
character and was defeated. Margaret stuck to her guns as
she was always to do in future. Once she had grasped her
laugh she never let it go; a rare phenomenon, for most
actresses in the course of a run sometimes flag or mistime,
but in all the shows I did with her, *she never let up.*

She was equally determined in the first film we under-
took together, a screen version of *Monday Night at Eight,* a
very funny backstage farce in which she played the playwright and of which one was constantly reminded in watching the currently very successful *Noise Off,* now [in 1982]
at the *Savoy."*

Later in Edinburgh on tour with *Short Story,* Eric Keown
told us that when Margaret was "making her entrance one
night through French windows, for the first time, excitedly
she felt a wave of sympathy from the audience that seemed
so solid that she felt she could almost touch it."

According to Keown, it was during this period in her life
that the screen also discovered Margaret Rutherford. "It began to dawn on the makers of films that the strange nonsense
lurking behind her tweeded respectability was a heaven-sent
gift to the screen."

She flew down from Scotland (her first plane trip) to make
a screen test for director Bernard Vorhans, who was planning
to film *Dusty Ermine.* She got the part, flying daily from
Edinburgh to London, then hurrying to the studios to shoot
her scenes. She always managed to get back to Edinburgh in
time for *Short Story's* evening performance.

"Thank God for fine weather," she said. "I was always able
to make divine connections."

Her role as Miss Butterfly, who coshes a detective with a lead-filled umbrella, so delighted the director that every day he gave her fresh lines to lengthen the part.

Margaret liked the challenge of the cinema: "I found it lonely work on the set, but the need to be precise, to remember that minute changes of expression would be visible to everyone and not merely to the front row of the stalls, appealed to me."

Besides, the extra money was a god-send. She treated herself to the first of a long line of green woollen capes and a rather large antique gilt Regency mirror with tiny whitish glass lilies popping out of every corner. Surveying the new acquisition for the first time in Margaret's bed-sitting room, Elizabeth, the maid, sagely observed: "Missy, isn't that too big for our lavatory?"

Dusty Ermine was followed by the housekeeper's role in *Talk of the Devil,* directed by Carol (later Sir Carol) Reed, whom she called "a charming young man," and a part in *Beauty and the Barge,* in which she appeared with another master of comedy, Gordon Harker.

"In filming," said Margaret, "I found myself constantly grateful that I had learned elocution and knew how to use my voice, even in a mere whisper."

During the two years that followed, with brief breaks for boating with Stringer in his mother's rowboat, Margaret appeared in three plays, the first of which, *Farewell Performance,* at the Lyric, was true to its name, folding after nine days.

Back she went to her favorite Embassy Theatre at Swiss Cottage for *Tavern in the Town* by Arthur Macrae and *Up the Garden Path* by John Ireland Wood, both directed by Murray Macdonald.

Of Aunt Bella, Margaret's role in *Tavern in the Town,* Eric Keown wrote that it "at least gave Margaret Rutherford a chance to spread herself as a petulant aunt behind the bar, and to demonstrate her special ability to get fun out of a testy character and yet remain likable in herself."

Ivor Novello, Britain's incomparable star of musical comedy ("We'll gather lilacs in the rain again"), paid her a surprise visit after the performance, offering to buy *Up the Garden Path* for the West End. Unfortunately some others in the cast were not free to go, so the idea was dropped. However, it marked the beginning of a happy platonic friendship between Margaret and Ivor, and one that Stringer did not have to worry about. From that day until his death, Ivor affectionately called Margaret "Big Sister."

In *Melody That Got Lost,* the ingenious Phoenix Theatre production by C. Denis Freeman and Katherine North, adapted from Kjeld Abell's original, Margaret's role as the mother did not go unnoticed. After seeing her in it, novelist M. J. Farrell (pen name for Molly Keane) and actor John Perry, the co-authors of *Spring Meeting,* sent a script for her to read, saying they had been impressed with her "sensitive" performance. Farrell and Perry, thinking they had written a very funny play, were surprised when, after reading their script, Margaret declared: "Oh no, people won't laugh at Aunt Bijou Furze. They shouldn't, should they? She is such a tragic character."

Molly Keane was just right for Margaret Rutherford. Reviewing her novel *Good Behaviour* in *Newsweek,* June 15, 1981, Walter Clemons had this to say of her writings: "Nostalgia and hatred are inextricably mingled in Molly Keane's portrayal of a world of vanished grace, fun and cruelty."

He also makes note of the fact that "she [Molly] was a popular playwright whose 'Spring Meeting' made a star of Margaret Rutherford in 1938."

It was Tyrone Guthrie who had asked the authors to consider Margaret for the role; John Gielgud was the director. Gielgud was the man Stringer most admired throughout his life.

The story concerned an impoverished Irish family whose baronet head had spent a fortune on horses and old brandy while his two unfortunate daughters had each to make do on a skimpy annual allowance of only twenty-five pounds. Aunt Bijou was a seventyish lady who was not quite right in the head. She loved nothing more than to bet on horses, her turf adviser being James, the household's general factotum.

At the Ambassadors Theatre on the first night, May 31, Margaret conquered the house with her entrance line spoken to the long-suffering James: "Skin on the milk and no biscuits!"

"The entire house simply rocked with laughter," said Mother, in recalling the glad occasion. "I have never thought of Aunt Bijou as being comical. But then I have also thought that a lot of comic characters I have played weren't funny either. To me a woman like Aunt Bijou had a deep streak of disturbing pathos that one finds often in the so-called comic characters of life."

Only Eric Keown, she thought, captured the true essence of her Bijou when he wrote:

> She meant much more in the play than just a comic aunt, because she stood as a symbol of everything her two all-but-trapped nieces were desperate to avoid; and it was Margaret Rutherford's triumph that while making her a devastating figure of fun she gave her at the same time an extraordinary sympathy, so that when she advised, "If a man you know to be common asks you to dance, my darlings, think a little and then say, 'no'," it was easy to see how much she privately regretted the toll of such inhibitions in her own life.

Next day the reviews of that "astonishing performance" gladdened Margaret's heart. Not only had she become a star in her own right after years of hard work and many disappointments, she was idolized by those all-important souls who loyally climbed the stairs up to the gallery. Always they left their autograph books for her to sign, together with the simple posies she most appreciated. Touched, she remarked: *"The Spring Meeting"* gallery appreciated what I was trying to interpret in poor Aunt Bijou and they gave me their unlimited affection because of it."

During the six months that she stayed with the cast (she always hated long runs), Margaret looked forward with relish to the bowl of hot porridge, which she obviously enjoyed, to the delight of the audience. She would immortalize the property manager for making it "without any of those disagreeable lumps."

It even replaced the cup of hot Bovril she would otherwise have taken in her dressing room, before going home to bacon and eggs, always a *must* after the theater.

London took Margaret Rutherford to its heart during that long, beautiful summer, although Stringer was somewhat taken aback to see a magazine cover showing his Margaret wearing a richly floral hat.

"Like a juicy slice from the seed catalogue," he slyly told her.

"I still felt that I had not yet met my testing part. And here it was; the incomparable Miss Prism in Oscar Wilde's *The Importance of Being Earnest*," Margaret later recalled.

She accepted "with joy" John Gielgud's offer to play in his new production. Gielgud had been greatly impressed with what he called "your own particular style of acting and your genius for filling out a small incident with a comic life of its own. This is why I knew that you were so right for Miss Prism."

Margaret liked working with Gielgud because Stringer admired his work so much, both as actor and director. She knew that he was not merely being flattering when he said, "When I went to see *Hervey House* I was struck by your performance as the duchess. I had also heard of you making a great success with Marie Tempest and that you had had a tussle with her. She was a bit of a tartar and hadn't been pleased when you stole the show in *Short Story* in the first scene. . . . Marie had lost her husband by then and had become more gentle but was always a little arrogant until someone stood up to her."

Finding a full-page photograph of herself in the program, Margaret knew that finally she had *arrived* in the theater. As Eric Keown acknowledged: "It was by far the most important part she had yet played in the West End, and also the most difficult, for its traditional outlines left little room for fresh creation."

Gielgud cast himself as John Worthing; Edith Evans, who was far from mute this time, played Lady Bracknell; George Howe was an inspired choice to play Canon Chasuble to Margaret's delicious Miss Prism. Their scenes together were charmed.

The play opened for eight charity performances in January 1939 at the Globe, after which it went into cold storage until August. Little did Mother think that one day a sensitive portrait of her by Michael Noakes would hang in the foyer of that same theater.

"Again that feared pen of James Agate scampered into print," wrote my mother. He criticized much of the production in the mighty *Times,* but not the individual performances of the Misses Evans and Rutherford! Of Margaret's, he said: "She could not miss perfection if she aimed wide of it . . . Miss Margaret Rutherford's bridling over the restored handbag, as if it were a favorite cat long lost and now astonishingly mewing in her lap, being as restrained and effective a piece of drollery as one could wish for."

August was a bad month for the reopening, with talk of war everywhere. When hostilities were finally declared, all the London theaters closed down early in September, but

The Importance of Being Earnest was later revived for a short run at the Golders Green Hippodrome.

During this period an antique chair broke on stage under the formidable Miss Prism's weight, sending her into the startled arms of Canon Chasuble, again played superbly by George Howe (brother of Bea Howe, author of scholarly works on Victoriana). They released "helpless giggles." Margaret made no excuse for her own laughter: "I did the natural thing and of course, the audience loved it!!" (Years later she experienced a repeat performance of the same traumatic collapse in the same play in Canada, when another genuine antique chair full of dry rot simply disintegrated beneath her.)

By this time Margaret had undergone some changes in her personal life. Elizabeth Orphin, the second-sighted maid, had grown too old to look after her and had somewhat reluctantly retired to her little "doll's house cottage; one room up and another down," Number Nine, Golden Terrace, in the seaside town of Dawlish, Devon. This, as Margaret said, "was filled to the brim with possesions that she had collected or had been given her." She would always look upon her Missy as the daughter she had never had and also as a replacement for "the two dear boys that I lost." She wrote Margaret at least twice a week, being the confidante in the long-term romance with Stringer Davis that would last fifteen years! For his part, he often joked that "Elizabeth did most of Margaret's courting."

Elizabeth's home was also a haven between plays when Margaret needed a rest. As it was too small to accomodate them both comfortably, Margaret would stay close by at the Queen's Hotel, taking long walks to enjoy her beloved sea breezes, and always returning to Nine Golden Terrace in time for tea, after which Elizabeth would read Missy's tea-leaves in the empty cup. She was very serious about this mystical accomplishment, but refused to read "Mr. Davis's because he says that I cheat and move the tea-leaves with my knitting needle so that everything comes out all right."

Stringer had always been a welcome if hungry visitor when he visited Margaret while Elizabeth was looking after her. Elizabeth would recall these visits in a letter to "my dear Missy." "I often think of Mr. Davis how he used to enjoy all I cooked for him. . . . He never left anything on his plate, did he?"

Margaret now lived with her stand-in and close friend, Grace Bridges, an understanding if sometimes exasperated lady. Even then life with Margaret Rutherford could be strenuous but never dull. It wasn't everybody who had the energy after a hard day's work to get up out of a warm bed in an unheated bedroom and take part in breathing and "straightening-the-back" exercises.

Mother gave deep thought as to what her contribution should be toward helping the war effort. "I worried immensely about what I could do. . . . I was not trained for canteen cooking; I had no practical nursing experience. It seemed to me the best thing was to try and make the public laugh and forget their worries." As it turned out, she was probably right.

She had quite a shock when her Stringer, than all of forty years old, volunteered for the army. All his life he was super-patriotic and at that time it seemed the only right thing to do. Away he went to Beverley, Yorkshire, to train as an officer, writing Margaret (he never called her Peggy) on October 18:

> Time is more precious to me than in any Repertory Company. We're doing a fortnight's intense course so I'm sorry I can't write letters or I'll never catch up. . . . My saluting is very *nearly* un-selfconscious! I believe I really am beginning to get the hang of the Bren Gun & can take it to bits and *nearly* put it together again! My Drill is terrible. . . . My Bayonet Fighting is a nightmare of misplaced enthusi-

asm. I nearly lost a foot today and my lungs will never be the same again. Our Sergeant Instructor is charming & muddles his left & his right hands! Please send me an arty photograph of yourself; such as you have made for the programmes.

She sent him the photograph, in addition to piles of *Illustrated London News,* which he never had time to read; clean handkerchiefs, as he was always catching colds; and the most expensive Turkish cigarettes, for which he had an affinity. In addition, Elizabeth deluged him with cans of clotted Devonshire cream, homemade marrow jam (his favorite), and countless pairs of khaki socks that she had knitted. His official and unofficial girlfriends sent him so much homemade soup that once, after leading a church parade, he had enough to warm up the entire platoon!

Proudly Margaret mailed on for Elizabeth to read his letter in which he could now proudly boast:

I am a First Class Shot! Nobody more surprised than myself—the first two targets I fired for practice before the test began were *dreadful,* but I seemed to get my eye in and passed by the comfortable margin of three Bulls!

We dug trenches for three hours in a blizzard however and I did *not* distinguish myself—I gave in completely when we were suddenly told to put gas masks on. I had rather a nasty cold, but the extreme exertion seems to have made it better. *Now* we have been double inoculated, once in each arm, and await any interesting results. Black Thursday and Black Friday!

As a postscript he appreciatively added: "Many thanks for your posh cigarettes. I smoke as I write, and they were enviously admired by my Brother Officers." He was now Second-Lieutenant James Buckley Stringer Davis.

Although Margaret hated violence or cruelty in any form, she finally agreed to play Mrs. Danvers, the sinister house-

51

keeper in the Queen's Theatre production of Daphne du Maurier's *Rebecca*. Margaret explained:

> I knew in my heart that Mrs. Danvers did appear evil and maleficent, but I tried to see her differently. Of course I had to make Mrs. Danvers a terrifying dragon, but I wanted my audience to understand why she was so deeply motivated by hate. It was the kind of psychological problem that appears in many disguises in life. . . . In any case, the play was a winner from the start, adapted, as it had been, from a best-selling novel with plenty of woman appeal.

Writing from her home, Kilmarth, Par, Cornwall, on November 10, 1982, Dame Daphne du Maurier agreed wholeheartedly with the Rutherford interpretation of the housekeeper. It was, she said, "true to the book."

Stringer was pleased that she had what he called "such a meaty role." Writing on stationery from the Royal Station Hotel, Hull (he had gone there for a hot bath, which he thought might kill or cure one of his perpetual colds), Stringer commented: "I see from today's *Observer,* which I read for quite 3 minutes before I was called away & somebody pinched it, that 'Importance' goes on & also 'Rebecca' is announced."

A little wistfully and probably homesick for the old theatrical life, he added: "I heard Raymond [Huntley] in 'Mary Rose' over the wireless the other night (just a bit before a meal) and I didn't think he was *quite* as good as *I* was!"

After the heartwarming Miss Prism, the wicked housekeeeer role provided a great challenge. Keown said: "Margaret Rutherford generated uncanny menace. Wherever poor little Mrs. de Winter crept away for a momentary breather, she was sure to find the evil face of the obsessed housekeeper glowering behind her."

She played Mrs. Danvers throughout that harrowing summer, a time of blackouts, bombings, and gas masks. With her deep sensibility, the strain of portraying the monstrous Mrs. Danvers was almost too much. Then, when the play was on tour in Exeter, Noel Coward and Hugh "Binkie" Beaumont appeared like two fairy godfathers to offer her the role of Madame Arcati, the genial medium in *Blithe Spirit!*

Binkie was a law unto himself in the theater world. Playwright John Osborne, reviewing *The Noel Coward Diaries* in the *New York Times Book Review* of October 3, 1982, aptly called his domain *Binkiedom*.

Binkie seems to have liked Margaret right from their first meeting when she was an hour late for that audition. "Margaret was a very *human* being," he would one day tell Stringer.

Noel had been warned by Binkie that Margaret was sensitive and could be hurt easily. She had to be treated with kid gloves. Both men were of one mind that she *was* Madame Arcati and time proved them right. Now they had to sell her on the idea, so first of all they treated her to a good supper. Afterward, Noel began to read his work, while she, poor soul, grew sleepier and sleepier. All she wanted was to go to bed, but Noel Coward was not the sort of person to be put down.

"I had often heard," she said, "that when crossed, he could be rather biting. I did not wish to be rude . . . Mrs. Danvers had simply worn me out for the evening."

Good manners and common sense prevailed as they always did with Mother, and she forced herself to rise to the occasion. As Noel read the final lines, both he and Binkie looked expectantly for her instant reaction. They were both surprised when she announced quite firmly—and she could be very firm at times—that she, Margaret Rutherford, had a great respect for professional mediums, many of whom she believed to have genuine spiritualistic gifts. For that reason she refused to be a party to hurting or making fun of them. Instead she would have to play Madame Arcati "straight."

With that volley she politely made her excuses and went

up to bed, leaving Noel Coward for once speechless. Years later he would laugh over the incident and tell her: "You *were* Madame Arcati. You *were* dazzingly funny; the greatest comic performance of your career."

She did not see it as funny and insisted that when the time came, the epitaph "A Blithe Spirit" should be inscribed upon her tombstone.

Margaret continued to share her day-to-day trials and tribulations with Stringer, and he with her. She was invited to become an honorary vice-president of the British Star Club, which, as the secretary, Cecil A. Kitson, wrote her, "is made up of intelligent film- and-playgoers."

In turn, Stringer wrote: "Somehow, having volunteered and been *accepted,* and to feel myself not frightened of anybody, gives me an *irresponsibility* in such moments that is most enlightening. I think it must be something to do with age, and the fact that I'm only too willing to have my mistakes pointed out and corrected."

His descriptions of army life continued to amuse her (and Elizabeth):

> I made Regimental History today and practically broke up a Parade by calling the Regimental Sergeant Major, "Sir!!!" And talking of officers, there is a Senior Captain who is fearsome of aspect with a red bristling moustache. I have not come under his command yet—he commands the Company which is in Beverley. He is quite the Fire-eater type, devouring Subalterns before breakfast. He is though—off stage—a very nice person, a fine man on or off duty.

They seem to have gotten quite friendly, for a few letters later Stringer told Margaret: "I am going to see 'Geneva' at Hull with our fire-breathing Commander, Captain *Spicer* (By Gad, Sir!). (Did I tell you that his moustache glows at *night*??"

Then he proudly informed her:

> I have invested in a Battle Dress to save my Beautiful
> Uniform on Field Work, Digging etc. I have also bought a
> Forage Cap (one of those Militia triangular affairs that slip
> about over one ear). I don't think you would like me in
> them very much—I look rather Common and am Inclined
> to Swagger!! On the other hand my New Regimental But-
> tons, with their silver Centres are a *Dream*! I can now
> Turn About without wobbling—so we *shall* win the War
> after all.
>
> Now I'm going to read some Army Pamphlets—*engross-
> ing*! What style!! Did you know a Bomb has 'segmentation
> to assist fragmentation'? Ain't that 'succinct'?

He had a week's leave beginning December 30, and they
were able to meet. He was wearing the expensive wrist watch
that he had asked her to get him for Christmas. "I hardly like
to ask for it," he had written, because it *must be a good one.*
Luminous, *with* a secondhand and some sort of a grill or
guard. It's part of my equipment and must be storm-proof
and very reliable—so altogether it's rather a tall order."
She met his train in London, gave a small party for him,
and did her best to remain cheerful, for she guessed that he
would soon be going to the front. In between he had to go to
Bournemouth to see his mother. Somewhere along the line
Margaret and Stringer had a little falling out, probably due to
the uncertainty and tension of the times. Later he would
write her: "I'm going to forget all about the unhappy dramatic Margaret of Garlands Hotel, quite lovely though she
looked in her Frowning Jealousy, and remember only the
jolly journey and Sunday when we were as we have always
been—good friends in love, understanding and sympathy."
It was no secret between them that she was jealous of his
mother, but then that lady had been very unkind, referring to
her as "that older actress woman you have been seeing over
the years." She did not like his men friends either.

"I may come quite close to you—I may go far away—I *might* come on leave unexpectedly any minute or may drag on months. One doesn't know—but I shall be thinking of you and egging you on in your Success," he told her. "Good luck and inspiration in *your* studies! Remember the common-sense and even humorous angle that needs balancing and compensating in these harsh, emotion-arousing characters!"

On May 3 he was in France and writing her that

> we had a good crossing and although we are under canvas and working hard at various labours we are fit and already getting that happy satisfied feeling of an inevitably tough job done as well as we can. . . . I'm doing a certain amount of manual labour with the troops to encourage them and harden *me*. I am getting to throw a pretty shovelful! I can tell you nothing of what part of France I am in . . . just "Somewhere"—but it's beautiful in its Spring foliage, and we've had some lovely sun—also thunder & a bitter east wind—quite like England!

Although she was very involved with tryouts and rehearsals for the London opening of *Blithe Spirit,* Margaret always found time to write him. She was very worried for his safety and communicated her worst fears to her letters. Gently he remonstrated with her: "They are dear letters, but Margaret dear you make yourself *suffer* so! God knows there are horrors & risks enough without rushing in imagination to meet them. I definitely bar sentences like 'I can't bear to *think* what horror—etc—etc.'"

Along with other such stars as Joan Crawford, Bette Davis, and Mae West, Margaret Rutherford was now a prime subject for stage impersonators. Stringer then mentioned that "it must have been a curious experience seeing your first Impersonation (I mean Robert Helpman). I expect one's reaction is something like, "Yes, that's all very obvious, but it's not as easy as all that!!"

Stringer's overseas stint lasted scarcely a month, finally turning into a nightmare. On May 28, exposed by the capitulation of the Belgians, the British expeditionary force of some 250,000 had to be withdrawn, chiefly from the beaches of Dunkirk.

"We marched backwards & forwards *all* over France & Belgium, he wrote,

> always zig-zagging away from the Front line as we thought, until it closed in on us. We repeatedly did rear-guard action, and were incessantly under fire. Absence of information, and the extreme scarcity of Orders of any sort from people above us, gave us rather a sneaking-unofficial kind of feeling. We were not, for example, just for a moment at all sure that we had not blown up a whole row of expensive bridges at the bidding of a Spy, rather than from one of our own Generals!

He was forced to burn the songs he had composed along with the mailbags. Margaret's love-letters together with a dozen cans of Elizabeth's clotted cream he lovingly buried. One wonders if, after the war, anybody ever found them.

By heroic efforts some 200,000 British and 140,000 French troops were rescued by June 4, and Stringer was among them. "I came through without a scratch," he said, "but was, I am afraid, completely exhausted by lack of food & sleep—the latter rather my own fault for fussing too much." He wired Margaret at the Queen's Theatre to come to the Green Room Club at 12:15 P.M., or to catch up with him as he boarded the Waterloo-Okehampton train, which left at 12:50.

Poor Margaret! Stringer had gotten his theaters mixed. Margaret had opened in *Blithe Spirit* the previous night at the Piccadilly. She was sleeping late in her room and didn't get his message until the next evening; by that time it was too late. Hurt by what he took to be her lack of interest "and still feeling a little bit of a hero," Stringer went home to his Mama and Aunt Paddy in Bournemouth, where he promptly came down with chronic bronchitis.

Noel Coward had directed his own play and, in spite of the war, the opening night was a brilliant social occasion. There was more of a spirit of relief than defeat that the boys had been rescued from Dunkirk.

Before the performance, Noel appeared in Margaret's dressing room to give her a present. It was a small teddy bear; knowing her passion for stuffed toys, he thought she would like it to remember the occasion. She promptly christened the bear Noel with a teaspoonful of hot Bovril. Today the little fellow is enjoyed by year-round visitors to the Theatre Museum, Boothbay, Maine, where Franklyn Lenthall, godfather to Margaret's granddaughter, Natasha, is the curator.

Needless to say, *Blithe Spirit* was to be one of Noel Coward's best-loved plays and for Margaret perhaps her most famous role. "It was wonderful cycling through the woods this evening. I was deafened with bird song!" Madame Arcati's opening lines never failed her. "It was sheer joy to hear my audience laughing and sighing with happiness."

She played Madame Arcarti "straight and for real," just as she had told Noel and Binkie that she would, and she had been correct. "So to get my business right I had a private sitting with a famous medium before rehearsals even began."

Keown wrote favorably: "No-one who saw *Blithe Spirit* will forget the preposterous fervor (no doubt reinforced by the years of pedalling around Wimbledon) with which she dismissed the uphill disadvantages of the bicycle: 'Just knack again. Down with your head, up with your heart, and you're over the top like a flash and skimming down the other side like a dragonfly'."

Kay Hammond and Fay Compton were both sensational

too, with their green hair and mauve eyebrows. "Rex Harrison was the perfect foil for all three of us," said Margaret, "and this time I did not have to kick him. I loved to watch Kay and Fay cook up their paint mixture over a heater." The *Tatler*'s critic wrote:

> Miss Rutherford is not one of your pale anaemic dabblers in the psychic but a thoroughly hearty, bicycling *bon viveuse,* breathing deeply and skipping about with a triumph when she brings off a coup. To see her Madame Arcati get up from an armchair is a lesson in eccentric observation. To hear her tra-la-la-ing in the hour of victory is to assist at a comic inspiration of the first order.

At a genuine psychic luncheon Margaret was delighted to be the guest of honor of a group of professional mediums. They were full of praise for the way she had portrayed one of their kind. Margaret gratefully told them she had played the role with understanding because "I had no right to make fun of sincere professional mediums."

Blithe Spirit, however, had its detractors, as Margaret's long-time friend, Elfrida Down Kettleborough, recalls: "Peggy enjoyed it. To some it was hilarious, but others who had recently lost relations kept writing to her, accusing her of tampering with the spirit world. She was a very sensitive person and understood their feelings."

In researching this book I found only one disturbing note concerning her actual playing of the role; it appeared in *The Noel Coward Diaries,* edited by Graham Payn and Sheridan Morley, published by Little, Brown in 1982.

The entry for July 12, 1941 reads: "Saw part of *Blithe Spirit.* Good house. Performance all right except for Margaret Rutherford."

After his telling her on several occasions that she *was* Madame Arcati, it did seem to be rather two-faced. Writing Joan D. Hirst, who looks after the Noel Coward Estate in London,

I received the following reply: "I am afraid I cannot help you over the entry in the 'Noël Coward Diaries.' I can only say that the diaries were published with the minimum of editing (taking out repetitions, etc.) and that Noel was very fond of your Mother, and admired her work."

Blithe Spirit ran for 1,997 performances, Margaret staying with the cast just over twelve months, a record in itself for her, as she hated long runs. For the rest of her life and even afterward, she would be the original *Blithe Spirit*.

Romantically the picture was not so rosy. Stringer, recovering from his cold, did not visit her once during his post-Dunkirk leave, nor did he come to see her in her greatest triumph to date . . . at least not then. He was content to sulk with his indulgent Mama, watching Harris, the gardener, clip the hedge. To add insult to injury, when he did leave home, before returning to his new billet in Cornwall, he visited several of his old male cronies in the theater.

Margaret was deeply hurt; Elizabeth was outraged. "What can you expect with a Mother like her who is so envious towards you," she wrote her beloved Missy. "His Mother had done this to you, so let the scales fall from your dear eyes but treat him with not a smile."

Margaret took Elizabeth's advice and for a while completely ignored Stringer, who was quick to take the hint, but appears not to have been the least bit repentant:

> As you're in an emotional mood I'm afraid it's more than I can stand to see you. . . . I don't care one blue pencil whether I'm "a man" or not—I'm going out & I want some cheerful society. I freely admit that I want to see Osmund, Raymond and Winnie as well as you . . . and I'm not going to be made shamefaced over it.

Whether he did go and see the mysterious Osmund, Raymond, and Winnie, I don't know, as they had long disappeared from our family story when I came on the scene. That he took his Mama and Aunt Paddy to see *The Light of Heart* in Bournemouth is a fact. He also leaves rather a revealing word-picture of his mother at this late period in her life:

"Mother likes Bournemouth in spite of the air-raid alarms. She derives great comfort from being amongst real gentlefolk and feels content. The great point is that in Bournemouth *her class & type* predominate, and will be sympathetically handled by the authorities."

Elizabeth continued to give advice and at the same time plan the reconciliation. She made her Missy an apple-green "bathing dress" so that "Mr. Davis can see your beautiful figure and white skin." They both promised Margaret's ex-maid that they would meet at their favorite trysting spot by the River Thames. There Elizabeth's apple-green bathing dress seems to have triumphed: The long-running lovers kissed and made up! This was the only recorded quarrel that they ever were to have. After that, whenever Margaret felt upset she would retire to her bedroom with Minnie the stuffed mouse. Minnie was always understanding and could not answer back!

Elizabeth often wrote Margaret to take a rest. "Go to Oxted and see your Benn aunty." This was Aunt Rene, her father's sister, and it was to Aunt Rene that she turned when, like a voice from the past, she received the letter from his friend, C. H. Gilpin. Gilpin had also written: "I only learned recently that you were the 'Peggy' who was so constantly in his thoughts & of whom he used to talk with much love. How thrilled he would be at the success which your talent has so justly brought you."

William Rutherford, Margaret's father, had, during his penitential period, nursed Gilpin through an attack of fever in Madras. Later, during the long, terrible years in the criminal insane asylum, Gilpin had visited him regularly.

Margaret had never fully recovered from the shock she

had undergone as a teenager when the old tramp had told her that her father was still alive. Any communication concerning him, however kind, made her nervous and uneasy. The public was fickle; what if they should find out Margaret Rutherford's true background? Would she be branded a murderer's daughter in the London tabloids?

Aunt Rene, as always, was reassuring. Writing from her home, Wayside, Blue House Lane, Oxted, Surrey, on February 20, 1940, she says:

> Darling One:
>   Your enclosed letter brought a choke in my throat. Gilpin as Dada [Margaret's father] used to call him was one of his choicest friends & a sweet soul. I remember his bringing his bride-to-be to see him when he was staying with me, & they made a lovely pair. I'm so glad he came to see you [act]. He must have felt the loving atmosphere round you. I hope you will see him in person some time. He comes of Quaker Stock I think.

Aunt Rene closed with "special remembrances to Elizabeth & Janie" (Janie was Margaret's esteemed Cockney dresser at the theater).

Writing from the House of Commons, Cousin Tony Benn tells us more of Aunt Rene. Says he:

> She was my great aunt who was known affectionately as Tweenie. She was the sister of William Rutherford and the daughter of Julius and lived until the end of the war [World War II]. Tweenie was a very kindly old lady and I remember her most vividly.
>   She was also very fond of your Mother Rutherford and at Christmas Mother Rutherford used to come to our family parties every year before the war. At that time she was teaching elocution and it used to be known that she hoped to get on to the stage but as she must have been in her late forties or early fifties, nobody really believed that she was

going to succeed in doing it. The tremendous success of her stage debut just before the war took the whole family by surprise.

Blunt House was the home of my Uncle Ernest Benn, brother of my father, and himself the son of John Williams Benn who was the brother of William Rutherford.

On the Nicholson side of the family, Margaret heard regularly from that same Cousin Muriel who was so anti-theater when they were children that she had to be shut in a cupboard during the performances. Muriel now lived appropriately in a place called Duvsland. From there on June 15, 1940, she wrote a foreboding letter to Margaret to tell her that "the nations are indeed being 'gathered together' and we are now paying for all our wrong doing. . . . This may be the 'last days' and this all the beginning of Armageddon."

She then asked the busy Margaret if she would kindly help her sell the family silver, as she had "only been offered thirty-five shillings for the lot," and at the same time advised Margaret to make her will!

"I think one ought to make a will," she continued.

I have kept putting off the evil day—but it is not fair to those who are left behind & have to clear up one's business. I shall leave to you my share of 2 St. John's [the house at Wimbledon, which their Aunt Fan had left them jointly, charging at the same time that she wished them to cremate her as cheaply as possible] although at present it must be a drop in the ocean, yet the future is so uncertain, one may be thankful of literally every penny. . . . Is there anything you would especially like, in case I am disposed of before you are—e.g., any of the furniture which came from Wimbledon such as Aunt Annie's writing table. . . ? I don't suppose for one moment I shall be allowed to "go" until I have at least lived my three score years and ten! but one must be practical—it is about the only thing left for one to do!

She ended the letter rather ominously: "You will take all precautions, won't you?"

The war years continued . . . Stringer was attentive . . . Elizabeth continued her match-making: "You need a good man to take care of you . . ." she kept writing Margaret, at the same time keeping up Stringer's flowing stream of clotted cream. She wanted to see her Missy settled before she died. The aches and pains became more constant; Margaret would send money to buy her little extras. "I had to get myself a little drop of gin. Thought it would clear my bladder, which it did. . . . Thank you for sending me the postal order . . ."

Margaret was always thoughtful; she loved giving presents. For Christmas of 1941 Aunt Rene received a pretty pink primula; when writing to thank her niece, she mentioned that "Will & family are popping in & out most days & make a happy interlude. How do you like having a lord for a cousin, darling? His proud old Aunt is feeling especially privileged being in such close touch with him just now. If you manage to come along while they are at Blunt House we will get together for a rejoicing. I think I told you they were there as paying guests, didn't I?"

Will, now the first Lord Stansgate, was cousin Tony Benn's father. He had served in dangerous guerilla activities during the Gallipoli landings in the First World War and later in authorized privateering in the Red Sea. He had accepted a viscountcy that same year because the Labour Party, which he had represented for years as a Member of Parliament, wanted more representation in the House of Lords. His new title, which obviously delighted Aunt Rene, was Viscount Stansgate of Essex.

Margaret was now much in demand, taking small parts in two films. The first was *The Demi-Paradise,* directed by Anthony Asquith, made when the wartime Anglo-Russian alliance was in full flower. Laurence Olivier played to distinction the Soviet officer posted in England, with Margaret portraying Rowena Ventnor, lady bountiful of the village in which he finds himself. She discovered the future Lord Olivier to be "nice and friendly." He told her: "I've been in films four years now and I'm just getting the knack."

Afterward, when times seemed dark, she often repeated the lines he spoke in *The Demi-Paradise:* "They [the English] have developed a religion of making the best of things, and their sense of humor is the guiding spirit of their lives."

Margaret also agreed to a one-day role in *The Yellow Canary.* She was so good that Herbert Wilcox, the director, enlarged her part so that she found herself working for three weeks.

It was the story of German U-boats and a British convoy. Wilcox, Anna Neagle's husband, proved a sympathetic director, letting her do all the chin wigglings and hand flourishes that had become her peculiar trademark. Later he wrote her: "I have never met anyone in my long experience so completely camera and audience unconscious, and this is also why you are such a rare personality."

Margaret always liked to improvise. As the eccentric old lady she spontaneously gave the Nazi officer a sharp kick on his ankle. Wilcox left it in the movie while Margaret slyly commented: "I was tempted to kick his bottom but that would have been most unlady-like!"

Then, as a peeress, she had to compete with a flock of migratory birds in Harold French's *English without Tears.* "Give them their heads" she snapped, and they will do their stuff while I get on with my acting."

In September of 1944 she joined Ivor Novello, Diana Wynard, Gertrude Lawrence, and Jessie Matthews on an ENSA (Entertainments National Service Association) tour of British airfields and units in Normandy and Belgium. They were a very compatible and professional group. Jessie's nerves gave way when she saw the embarkation gangplank, crying out to Margaret that she couldn't climb "that thing."

Miss Rutherford took control in her best schoolmarm manner: "In situations like this there is simply nothing to do but make a firm stand and take control. Put your hands on your hips and then off you set, left, right, left, right . . . up the plank! *Jessie did as she was told.*"

Traveling by day and setting up their impromtu stages at night, the troupe found life full indeed. While the other ladies sang and performed comic skits, Margaret brought the house down with her Edward Lear poems. Ivor Novello sang his new song, "We'll Gather Lilacs," which later would take on a special significance for Margaret and her adopted children. Stringer never let a teatime pass without playing it!

Charmed with the Royal Air Force, Margaret took up a kind of flying herself, appearing as the White Queen, a role in which she alternated with Dame Sybil Thorndike for Clemence Dane's clever adaptation of Lewis Carroll's *Alice in Wonderland.* This was at the Palace Theatre in December 1944, with her old friend Esmé Church directing.

Calling Dame Sybil "a proficient aeronaut who could fly in and out of the wings on the wires with ease," Margaret confessed to having had to learn her flying "from the ground up." Once she had mastered the art of landing gracefully instead of bouncing, she gamely said: "It was one of the major thrills of my life. I used to look forward to my daily flight."

Then in 1945 *Blithe Spirit* was filmed at Denham under the able direction of David Lean.

With Rex Harrison again playing the much married widower-husband, Kay Hammond and Constance Cummings his ghostly wives, and Margaret repeating her Madame Arcati, it was destined to become a screen classic. There was even a remarkable parrot, who liked to upstage her with its screams of "Pretty poltergeist," to share Madame's red brick villa. Still a one-woman armada, Margaret used no stand-in for her hearty bicycle rides through the green Kentish countryside.

She thoroughly enjoyed the cucumber sandwiches, which as the medium she ate "to keep up my ectoplasmic strength."

Filming seemed unending, taking all of six months. She explained why: "Something to do with color film, which was then fairly new, having to be sent to America to be processed and then returned each time to match up. We all became very tired of it towards the end."

Time and Tide's was an important review:

> If you are not careful the old thing will materialize a whole "hockey team," and one saw what she meant. But it's not the arty-craftiness and the heartiness that Margaret Rutherford gets so right, it's the faith behind them. In the mad world in which all the characters find themselves after Elvira had materialized, Madame Arcati is the sanest and most purposeful character. She is also extremely resourceful. Observe her mounting the steps and declaiming rather insulting medieval rhymes while she shakes herbs over the phantom Ruth and Elvira. If any acting could be too good, hers would be *too* good.

Years later Constance Cummings told Margaret: "You were extraordinary. Partly it was because your own spiritual beliefs gave the part a great clarity and simplicity which made it so riveting. We weren't seeing an actress being funny. We were really seeing Madame Arcati!"

·5·
The Bride

AFTER a fifteen-year courtship it seemed logical for the lovers to get married. Elizabeth's clotted cream and bathing-dress had paid off at last. Besides, Mama Davis had passed away, leaving Stringer a houseful of furniture and her painted portrait. "One can only hope," mused Margaret, "that Mrs. Davis finds heaven as congenial as she did Bournemouth."

Stringer had been down to see the old family home near Reading for the last time [his mother had been evacuated to Bournemouth because of the war], since it had just been sold. Peering into the boathouse he found the rowboat just as Margaret and he had left it years before, when they had romantically called it their Venetian gondola.

Margaret was busy rehearsing for the part of Lady Charlotte Fayre in her favorite Ivor Novello's new musical, *Perchance to Dream*. She was sharing a flat in Beaconsfield, Buckinghamshire, with Grace Bridges ("dear Grace was better at coping with housework than I was"); getting out of the train one night she found Stringer standing on the platform. They walked arm-in-arm back to Margaret's home where, right in the hallway before she even had time to put down her hand-bag, Stringer fell on one knee (she thought of the dashing Errol Flynn as Sir Walter Raleigh and herself as Elizabeth I) and rather poetically proposed!

"Wilt thou have this man to be thy wedded husband . . . for better or worse, for richer, for poorer, in sickness and in health?"

"Of course," she replied, rising to the occasion. "I would marry you even if you lived in a Bedouin tent."

Later she would say:

> Ours was one of those romances that took a long time to bloom. For many years he had his mother, whom he loved dearly, to consider and I had my career. It was the war separation that changed everything. Tuft suddenly realized that there is nothing worse in life than loneliness and that perhaps after all he might be husband material. It took him all that time to find himself in that respect, if you see.

Stringer gave her a solitaire diamond engagement ring; when she later lost it in Australia, he replaced it with a large blue aquamarine in an antique filigree setting.

Janie, the Cockney dresser, had retired, so the first to hear the good news was her successor, the congenial Blanche Wright, wife of Bill Wright, Ivor Novello's personal valet and dresser for over twenty years. It was Ivor who had ar-ranged Blanche's introduction to Margaret. "Blanche," he had said, "I want you to dress a charming and adorable lady." Fortunately the two women liked each other immediately.

Said Margaret:

> Blanche was all that embodied the loyalty and devotion of real theater people. She cherished but never fussed me. She was one of the original French Cockaignes, a Miss

Lefèvre by name, coming from a family who had originally settled within the required sound of Bow Bells [the definition of a bonafide Cockney]. She came with a special recommendation from Ivor. Blanche, who spoke French with a real Cockney accent, made the best onion soup I have ever tasted. The secret is that she never stinted on the Gruyere cheese that covered the little rafts of toast.

She watched over me with the ferocity of a lioness over its cub. Everybody was properly inspected before she would let them into my dressing room. Ivor and Tuft were her only exceptions.

Margaret was glowing as she marched on stage for rehearsal next day. *Perchance to Dream* was to open in two weeks so there was no time to be lost. They had to be married without delay. Pulling off her gloves, she was confronted by an empty finger! Blanche and Margaret glanced around the stage. The former began to make distressed noises.

"What is going on there?" demanded Ivor.

"Margaret has lost her engagement ring," shouted Blanche, by this time almost in tears.

"Stop the orchestra," ordered Ivor. "Everyone down on their hands and knees until we find it."

Fortunately at that moment Blanche thought to look inside the long period gloves Margaret had been wearing . . . and there it was!

The ceremony, which had several Rutherfordish touches, took place on March 26, 1945, in Beaconsfield Parish Church, with the Reverend Donald Nicholson, assistant curate, officiating. Lieutenant (he had been promoted) James Buckley Stringer Davis was resplendent in his army officer's uniform. He arrived somewhat jauntily at the church with his best man, Margaret's cousin John Nicholson from Yorkshire.

Then a London taxi pulled up (Margaret had insisted that its occupant take a taxi all the way from London, where she had duly arrived by train) and Elizabeth Orphin stepped out, dressed all in her best chocolate brown with a significant stuffed bluebird in her velour hat. She had an enormous floral spray of white rosebuds that Stringer had bought her, and she in return had brought him, all the way from Devonshire, two cans of his favorite clotted cream, which she handed to the astonished curate by the door. It was also Elizabeth's day; no substitute Mother of the Bride was ever happier when, fortified by her little drop of gin, she walked up the aisle.

Meanwhile at Margaret's flat, Grace Bridges was doing her best to get the bride to the church on time. There had been so many things to remember; Aunt Bessie's gold watch with the bow for something old; Aunt Rene's blue sapphire brooch, a Benn family heirloom; gloves for something new . . . which Margaret in her excitement had forgotten. Faithful Grace was sent post-haste to buy a pair.

The bride ("I felt I was by that time a little past the age for wearing white") chose a biscuit-colored coat and skirt, designed by Worth and costing forty pounds—a lot of money in those days—with hat to match covered with veiling and golden stars. She was given away by her cousin, Professor Graham Nicholson.

The bride and groom somehow became parted during the ceremony—how, neither ever satisfactorily explained to me—and Grace Bridges found herself again in the familiar role of stand-in, which was all very well until the minister, looking her straight in the eye, demanded: "Do you take this man to be your lawful wedded husband . . .?"

"I am not taking anyone," said Grace in a loud voice, grabbing the bride and pulling her into place beside Stringer. "Margaret, you ought to be here, not me." Even the minister couldn't stop laughing.

Later, after signing the register in the vestry, the newlyweds managed to emerge by the wrong door, where instead of being met by a shower of rice, they were confronted by a row of tombstones.

The curate, as is sometimes the case in the Church of England, discreetly presented the bridegroom with a little booklet dealing with the more physical aspects of marriage, while two of the curate's more experienced gentlemen friends, "drew a little diagram to help us." At least the marital booklet was a bit of a failure as, years later, when I walked out of Hastings Parish Church with my bridegroom, John-Paul Simmons, Father Stringer handed that same booklet to his new son-in-law with the words: "I hope that this helps you more than it did me."

A small reception was held at the nearby Bull Hotel. Later Mr. and Mrs. Stringer Davis caught the Gerrards Cross bus to go home to the bride's "doll's house with the blue front door," which she had bought as a wedding gift for both of them. It had Art Nouveau water lilies in the glass of one of the windows and a lilac bush, which Ivor Novello had given them, newly planted in the tiny garden.

Next day it was back to work for the bride, with more champagne, wedding cake, and flowers right on stage.

Although she had never before appeared in a musical, Margaret enjoyed the new challenge. Like a happy child, she said: "How I loved that sweeping velvet dress, the vivid green of an Irish spring, my elegant bonnet with its swirling green feathers, and the lorgnette I wore on a golden chain."

She had one particularly beautiful and nostalgic scene, in which, left all alone in the ballroom, she began to dance.

"I have always loved to dance and at that moment each night it seemed that I floated round the stage. The whole scene had seized my imagination. It was past any dream that I could have had."

Stringer had a special leave for opening night, April 21, 1945. He was now Entertainments Officer in his regiment and carried the theme song, "We'll Gather Lilacs in the Rain Again," back to camp to play to his men among whom Margaret now had a number of fans.

Critic John Agate seems always to have had a soft spot for Margaret. After her performance in *Perchance to Dream,* he complimented her on her "magnificent determination to stand no nonsense and deliver none." Then John C. Trewin of the *Illustrated London News* wrote:

> We have left Margaret Rutherford to the last. What in the world is she doing at Huntersmoon with that unquenchable sense of comedy and the voice that, like Byron's cocking of the pistol, is a "strange quick jar upon the air"? Her part hardly exists; but ingeniously she makes a personage of a phantom and at the end, in Mr. Novello's odd little ghost scene behind the gauzes, a phantom of a personage.

Perhaps the most understanding tribute came from Eric Keown, who would one day write an appreciative book on her theatrical career: "What she was doing, of course, was being romantic. She has always been that; the gentleness and sympathy that soften even such grotesque figures as Bijou and Arcati spring from it."

Ivor Novello felt terrible that he could not spare the bride for another three months so that she could have a honeymoon. Finally Stringer and she were able to enjoy one in Cornwall where, said he, "Margaret wore me out trying to find King Arthur's seat in the wilds of Tintagel Castle."

About the same time, after collecting it from the cleaners, the new Mrs. Davis left her expensive wedding outfit in a telephone box. It was never seen again.

Stringer hated leaving her to return to the army, for already he feared that somehow she would overwork. She had told him everything about her father and he only loved her the more. "Margaret really loved him, you know," Father Stringer told me. "He was such a sick man."

He was worried about the bad dreams that she had during those first months of their marriage, of the sudden screams in the night and the chaotic awakenings. He would hold her in his arms and wipe her tears. It was always the same—she had seen her father. . . . In the end would she go mad like him?

The doctor respectfully called it a form of melancholia.

Florence Nicholson Ruther-
ford, Margaret's mother.
*(Rutherford House, Hudson,
New York.)*

William Rutherford (born William Rutherford Benn), Margaret's ill-fated father. *(Rutherford
House.)*

Margaret aged
seventeen.
*(Rutherford
House.)*

Margaret in
1928. *John
Erith. (Ruther-
ford House.)*

ABOVE:
Aunt Bessie
Nicholson,
Margaret's
adoptive
mother.
*(Wimbledon,
Rutherford
House.)*

Margaret as a Scottish dowager with Danny Kaye and
Dana Wynter in *On the Double*, made in Hollywood.
Danny had a sense of humor that matched her own.
He kept pinching her under the table when they did
a banquet scene! (*The Theatre Museum, Boothbay
Maine.*)

Margaret with Robert Morley in *Murder at the
Gallop* (1963). Robert was a cherished friend
throughout her career. *The Theatre Museum.*

Margaret as Miss Marple
in *Murder Most Foul*
(1964). *(The Theatre
Museum.)*

Margaret and Stringer
during the filming of
N.B.C.'s *The Stately
Ghosts of England*. The
cloak she is wearing is now
in the Theatre Museum in
Boothbay, Maine. (*The
Theatre Museum.*)

Nelly and Doom Hall on Brighton Beach, Sussex. The twins later married brothers named Ticehurst. (*William R. Perkins Memorial Library, Duke University.*)

Isabel Lydia Whitney, a watercolorist of repute and America's first woman fresco painter. (*Rutherford House.*)

Margaret and Dawn discuss engagement rings at a prenuptial luncheon held in November 1969 at the Waldorf Hotel, London. (*Rutherford House.*)

Margaret toasts Dawn and John-Paul after their Hastings wedding. (*Rutherford House.*)

OPPOSITE PAGE, CENTER: Dame Margaret considered relaxation a necessity and was quite happy to sit down for a lemonade on Bexhill beach in Sussex with ten-year-old Tony Benn—better known these days as Anthony Wedgwood Benn, M.P.

OPPOSITE PAGE, BOTTOM: Cousin Anthony Wedgwood Benn, M.P., when he was Secretary of State for Energy. (*Joe Bulaitis. British Information Services.*)

Margaret (LEFT) at Elm Close talking to a friend about ghosts and the after-life. *(The Theatre Museum.)* (RIGHT) In the garden at Beecholme, Old Heathfield, Sussex. *(Roger Pain.)*

Margaret and Stringer at Elm Close. *(The Theatre Museum.)*

Margaret and Stringer in the dining room at Elm Close. The copy of the Mona Lisa is a souvenir from their film *Innocents in Paris*. (*The Theatre Museum.*)

Her Oscar on the mantelpiece, Margaret pokes the fire at Elm Close. (*The Theatre Museum.*)

Dawn and Natasha in Hastings, England, in 1979. (*Philip Savins.*)

Dawn at her parents' grave in St. James Churchyard, Gerrards Cross, Buckinghamshire. (*The Buckingham Advertiser.*)

·6·
Mrs. Stringer Davis

NINETEEN FORTY-SEVEN was a busy year, with Stringer home from the army for good. Margaret made two films: *Meet Me at Dawn,* about duelling in Paris, and *While the Sun Shines,* based on Terence Rattigan's successful play, in which she played a doctor. Then John Gielgud invited her to be in *The Importance of Being Earnest,* which he planned to take on a North American tour. When Edith Evans refused the role she had made so much her own, that of Lady Bracknell, Margaret was asked to replace her, in which part she was more than adequate. In New York, Brooks Atkinson saw the play at the Royale and wrote of her: "As the overbearing Lady Bracknell, Miss Margaret Rutherford is tremendously skillful; the speaking, the walking, and the wearing of costumes all gathered up into one impression of insufferability."

Canadian and American audiences took her to their generous hearts, and she immediately took them to hers. Offstage she cut quite a figure in the trouser-suit, as she called it, that her dressmaker had "conjured up from a green-striped yellow blanket." It was offset with green fluffy earmuffs.

When Stringer's bad head cold forced him to take a horse and carriage to the top of Mont Royal in Montreal, she walked, "for some of that good Canadian fresh air." She was rather surprised when a young man shouted to her: "Where's your bicycle?"

Margaret and Stringer never forgot the night they were walking home from the theater arm in arm, when a young man stopped his car, jumped out, and asked: "Pardon me, ma'am, but are you Margaret Rutherford?" Then, handing her one enormous red tulip, he said: "Enjoy this!"

She equally loved it when another American admirer called her unique face "an English muffin."

Her description in *Time* pleased and at the same time embarrassed her: "She is so British that by comparison with her, even John Bull seems the son of a miscegenetic marriage."

Both as a play and as a motion picture, *The Happiest Days of Your Life* proved to be just that to Margaret Rutherford.

It opened at the Apollo in March 1948 with Richard Bird directing; John Dighton had written her a part that was pure Rutherford.

Miss Evelyn Whitchurch (Margaret) is headmistress of a girls' school; through a mistake at the British Ministry of Devacuation, she is billetted at Hilary Hall, an all-boys establishment. The long-suffering boys' headmaster, Godfrey Pond, played in her own words "so superbly by George Howe," simply did not have a chance.

Eric Keown wrote:

> She passed over poor Mr. Pond like a trumpeting steamroller; no demand was too outrageous, no cunning too low. It was an unflaggingly funny performance, in her wildest vein; and yet, as always with her, disbelief was suspended,

so that for a couple of hours one would have been prepared to swear that here was a typical member of that notoriously hilarious body, the Headmistresses' Conference.

Opening with a pitched battle of lukewarm fishcakes, followed by treacle oozing mysteriously from the girls' bicycle toolbags, it was a play written for laughs.

Margaret's delight was increased by seeing Stringer cast in a very good role as a well-meaning clergyman with a habit for causing parent hysteria.

The principal schoolgirl was Molly Weir, whose acting ability was matched only by her proficiency at shorthand. She had in fact once been Great Britain's champion shorthand writer with a speed of three hundred words a minute. Stringer became so fascinated that he decided there and then to study shorthand, to help with the answering of his wife's now considerable fan mail.

The Happiest Days of Your Life produced splendid notices, including Stringer's favorite: "The palm goes to Margaret Rutherford as a headmistress before whom an atomic bomb might quail."

"Ruthless femininity," grumbled Mr. Keown.

The film version would not be made until 1952, with Alistair Sim in the role of the long-suffering headmaster. Frank Launder directed. Again *Happiest Days* was an enormous success, preserving, as well as adding to, the lunacy of the play. For the movie the boys' school was renamed Nutbourne College; the actual shooting took place at Byculla School in Hampshire. Actual Byculla students shared acting honors with those from the Corona Theatrical School. Said Margaret with some satisfaction: "They were all completely mesmerised by me as their headmistress and all obeyed me instinctively."

The marvelous Joyce Grenfell played the hockey-loving sports mistress. "The best argument for good Anglo-American relations," Margaret called Joyce, that other most British of actresses, yet one who had close family ties in Virginia.

After dubbing Alistair "with perhaps the exception of Lassie the Wonder Dog, the wickedest actor in captivity," film critic Paul Holt wrote of his film bout with Miss Rutherford: "The result of this contest is, therefore, happily a draw and no blood shows. But with any less talented a performer, massacre would have been done. The whole thing ends in a shamble of giggles with headmaster Sim wearing his exasperation as a halo and headmistress Rutherford looking like Queen Boadicea at a difficult dress fitting."

Two other films of equally good quality had come Margaret's fortunate way in 1948. The first was *Miranda,* directed by Ken Annakin, in which she played Nurse Cary whose unique patient, Glynis Johns, was in fact a mermaid.

According to the *Observer,* as the only trained hospital nurse sufficiently eccentric to be called onto the case with safety, Margaret greeted her new patient "with a yelp of rapture." The London Zoo sea lion's shocked look when Miranda intercepted and swallowed its breakfast fish was also one to remember.

Ironically, when the film reached New York, the American censors had moral qualms. They decided that to be allowed the benefit of a tail, a mermaid must be married! When Miranda's tail was snipped off by the censors, there was a minor Rutherford explosion. "Most confused thing," she snapped. "It's a wonder they didn't make her wear bloomers."

The second film was a gem of its kind; it still sees regular service on television. *Passport to Pimlico* cast Margaret wearing one of the long capes that would become her fashion trademark, as Professor Hatton-Jones, who discovers that London's Pimlico district is really a small island of foreign territory that, centuries before, belonged to Burgundy.

Keown called it "genuine cinema" and a film that "marked the beginning of a new school of British comedies."

That same year there was a happy event in the Benn family: Margaret's cousin Anthony Neil Wedgwood Benn, better known as Tony, who was attending Oxford University, met a tall, blonde American student from Cincinnati named Caroline DeCamp. She was vivacious, witty, sensible, and loyal, the perfect match for a debonair young man with political ambitions. They met one Monday and were engaged on the Saturday; it really was a case of love at first sight, and after her own prolonged courtship with Stringer, Margaret the born romantic, loved it.

The first DeCamp had come to America with the early Dutch settlers; in the decades that followed, the family had distinguished itself in its adopted country. Harriet Beecher Stowe wrote of the Cincinnati Slave Underground Railroad, an organization that helped fugitive Southern slaves in their flight to freedom in the North and in neighboring Canada. The DeCamp family had been ardent sympathizers, helping in this dangerous work, defying the Fugitive Slave Act.

As a young girl, Caroline had surprised her Republican and conservative parents by announcing that she was becoming a Democrat! She explained that she could not understand why some people could be rich and privileged while others were so poor.

Tony and Caroline (Carol to her friends) were married in Cincinnati in 1949, returning afterward to live in England. The following year Tony stood for Parliament, winning a seat in the House of Commons as the member for Bristol, Southeast. He had the distinction of becoming the youngest member of Parliament.

Cousin Margaret, noting his good looks, determined Benn chin, and fine diction said somewhat sadly: "Cousin Tony would have made an excellent actor but he chose to join the Labour Party instead."

The year 1950 was a busy one, for in addition to her evening performances as Madame Desmortes in *Ring Around the Moon*, translated by Christopher Fry from Jean Anouilh's original, at the Globe Theatre, she managed to make the film versions of both *The Happiest Days of Your Life* and *Her Favorite Husband*, directed by Mario Solditi.

In the latter, Robert Beatty had to smack Jean Kent's bottom, which so upset the sensitive censor that although the smack was allowed to remain, the sound was not!

While in Rome to play Jean's mother, even the overly polite Margaret lost her temper briefly when a large British lady descended like another battleship upon her while she was trying to manipulate, with true British awkwardness, a plate of Italian spaghetti. She was exhausted from a long day's shooting and in a foreign land at that.

"Dear Miss Rutherford," the interloper simpered, "just what do you think of the Coliseum?"

Harnessing her chins, my mother carefully laid down her fork, fixing the woman with a glare. Then she uttered one word: "Draughty!"

When first offered the old aunt's part in *Ring Around the Moon*, Margaret had some misgivings about taking the role until Stringer suggested that it was really "a sort of charade."

"Make believe it is Christmas come early this year with all the dear children dressed up."

She took him at his word, noting: "I have always loved Christmas and of course Tuft was right; he is *always* right. I began then to really enjoy it." Besides, as she was to find, Peter Brook "added his own particular style of magic."

Brook was very understanding, especially of her fears that the bathchair that she had to use throughout the play might crash into the orchestra pit. So he took her out "for a scrumptious repast of roast pork and applesauce," after which they talked the problem over. Later Stringer was dispatched posthaste to buy a new bathchair that was easier to control, which of course he did in his quiet, efficient way.

Oliver Messel's "Winter Garden" set was pure enchantment. Eric Keown called it "a pocket edition of the Crystal Palace."

With Paul Scofield and Claire Bloom as her co-stars, Margaret was in excellent company. As the interfering old aunt, she "puffed a cheroot with contempt," drowning out the taste with hot Bovril in the interval. She also made liberal use of a snuffbox, but did draw the line at taking the real thing. "It was," she said, "mercifully empty."

Said Eric Keown:

> She boomed with malice. I used the word "malice" advisedly. In a woman essentially so gentle, and in an actress who took such pleasure in the simplicities of *Perchance to Dream,* this ability to sting may seem a surprising weapon; but as she employs it, it is never ugly. It governs much of her best comedy, lending it astringency and holding the balance of eccentricity.

Critic Cecil Wilson called Margaret's Madame Desmortes "a wicked, intriguing old battleaxe who kept track of everyone's affairs from a highly mobile invalid chair." This amused Margaret, who had learned all the secrets of mobile invalid chairs from her Sunday runs with Aunt Bessie in the great marble cemetery at Wimbledon. When Queen Elizabeth, the Queen Mother, came to see *Ring Around the Moon,* Margaret whizzed backstage in her wheelchair, announcing, much to Her Majesty's amusement: "Such an honor, and the audience are working like Trojans."

This was the beginning of a very special friendship between my mother and individual members of the British Royal Family. She was particularly fond of Princess Margaret, whose triumphant tours of Canada and the West Indies as a young woman were all too soon forgotten in the sadness of much of her later life.

"I wish they would give her a governorship or something," Mother would often say. "Princess Margaret has real potential . . . Oh, what an actress she would have made!"

She saw everything in the light of the theater. Of the Queen and Prince Philip, who were always so kind to her, she often repeated: "They are on center-stage all of the time."

That same year Mother became Patron of the Compass Club, a home for wayward boys. In return she received a delightful letter from the club's leader, John Hibberd, which began:

> My dear Miss Rutherford (or can I call you Mum?),
>
> I am writing as one of your sons (I too have no mother— She died when I was born) to thank you once again for giving up your Sunday evening.
>
> We all enjoyed your visit immensely, & the boys are as proud as peacocks about you. All I can hope is that both you and your husband really did enjoy yourselves too, and that in time you will become proud of your naughty? sons.
>
> Sports day for the whole institution takes place Bank Holiday Monday during the afternoon. Parents & friends of the lads are invited. (When you see the parents—you quite often forgive the lads for being there.)

Margaret took her new position as "den mother" very seriously. She regularly sent tickets as rewards for some of "her sons" to see her act at the theater.

In 1951 she again briefly became a peeress as the formidable Lady Pond (no relation to the harrassed headmaster of *Happiest Days*) in *The Magic Box*. This was the British film industry's tribute to William Friese-Greene, their native photographer who was among the first to make animated pictures. With Robert Donat, that gentle actor, playing Friese-Greene, there were many famous guest stars who had too little to do. Margaret summed it all up as "a huge meringue hidden under layers of whipped cream. None of us liked the taste very much."

That same year she was to lose her good friend Ivor Novello. Margaret adored him, although, as she said, "he did like to stay in bed as long as possible in his gorgeous silk Art Deco pajamas." She always believed that everyone should be up with the lark, learning parts (herself), writing books (me), or growing roses, writing new songs, or practicing shorthand (Stringer).

Like two children, Margaret and Ivor enjoyed secret jokes while rehearsing in the theater. If the director complained, Ivor would threaten, "If you are not nice to us I won't give you a gorgeous first night present."

Margaret loved going to Ivor's garden parties, which sometimes, at least for Margaret and Stringer Davis, lasted several days. These were held at Redroofs, his country home, and were presided over by thoughtful Olive Gilbert, who not only appeared in Ivor's plays, but as Margaret noted, "kept the household wheels spinning."

Olive was always sure to have on hand a goodly supply of the gooey cream buns and cucumber sandwiches that Margaret loved so much. Ivor always said that he grew the cucumbers especially for her and she quite believed him.

Margaret still loved to swim, declaring that "the colder the water, the more bracing, dear heart." With Ivor in his gay West Indian swimsuit and faithful Olive attired in a Victorian bathing costume and carrying six hot water bottles, "just to warm the pool up, dears," Margaret was in good company. Always before going to Redroofs she made a special safari to her favorite Boots the Chemists in order to buy the brightest bathing cap with matching strap.

At the time of Ivor's sudden death, March 6, 1951, he was

discussing a new production to be called *The Lily of the Valley,* in which Margaret was to have played his sister.

Blanche Wright rushed over with the news. "He's gone; he's gone," she cried, throwing herself into Margaret's ample arms. Together they went next morning to the private mortuary chapel where he lay "looking remarkably young and ageless as he would wish to be, but minus one of poor Olive's hot water-bottles." Margaret, who placed a bouquet of red roses across his folded hands, knelt with Blanche and prayed. "He meant so much to me, to all of us," Margaret said.

Then, temporarily overcome by a fit of melancholia, she took to her bed, because, as she told a sympathetic Stringer: "After Aunt Fan's I vowed never to attend another cremation."

The year 1952 saw what Margaret Rutherford termed "my gallant failure." This was *Miss Hargreaves,* a play written by one of her dearest friends, Frank Baker, which in book form had been a bestseller. Artist Dod Proctor had given Margaret a copy thinking it might interest her. It did!

The story concerned two young men vacationing in Ireland who amuse themselves by mentally conjuring up the figure of a preposterous old lady complete with butterfly net and cockatoo. They call her a niece of the Duke of Westminster. When they return home to their quiet English cathedral town, Miss Hargreaves appears too. Directed by Joan Kemp-Welch, it opened at the Royal Court, then a theater club.

Margaret, who adored the world of fantasy, said: "I liked *Miss Hargreaves.* I did not have to identify myself with her because I felt just like her." The critics panned the play but not the star.

Critic Harold Hobson explained:

> The pity of it is that, but for Mr. Baker's need for rationalisation, we should have accepted his entire story, just as we accept the square root of minus one, and other things man-

ifestly absurd and illogical, for the sake of what they bring us. In this case, they brought us Miss Margaret Rutherford and a character, ridiculous, pathetic, poetic and irresponsible, which, had it been worked on with half the zeal the author has given to philosophy, would have yielded rich and rare pleasures. Even so, Miss Rutherford in full activity with butterfly net in a cathedral cloister, Miss Rutherford giving instructions for the sort of meal that has not been seen in England for nearly fifty years, Miss Rutherford reciting a piece of nonsense verse with a full appreciation of its absurdity, and yet with a strange music, were welcome things.

Her co-star, a cockatoo named Charlie, was recruited from the London Zoo and lived at the theater in the men's dressing room. Although he had the unfortunate habit of calling Miss Hargreaves "you old bitch," which certainly wasn't in the play, Stringer and Margaret became so attached to Charlie that they begged the Zoo to let them take him home for Christmas.

"Who would want to spend the holidays alone in the men's dressing room," argued Stringer, with Margaret chiming in: "Poor dear." Their request was granted.

My father always said that Charlie was the best Christmas guest that they ever had. "For one thing," said Father Stringer, "he was so appreciative of my cooking, eating not one, but four dinners that Christmas. You see, he had a particular passion for turkey."

Although *Miss Hargreaves* did not officially make the West End, "she" was by no means a failure in the provinces. For years afterward Margaret and the author, Frank Baker, were hoping to see it made into a film but it never was. However, more than once she told me that Miss Hargreaves would always be an important part of her life, perhaps because fantasy delighted her so much.

In spite of the *Miss Hargreaves* disappointment, 1952 was

one of her busiest years in the studio. She was in five different productions, the most important of which was Anthony Asquith's version of Oscar Wilde's *The Importance of Being Earnest*. It was said to have saved the critics' sanity at the Venice Film Festival. Margaret again played her beloved Miss Prism; her scenes, this time with Miles Malleson as Chasuble, were delicious. Edith Evans played Lady Bracknell, this time for a worldwide audience. Michael Redgrave as Earnest had that unforgettable scene with Miss Prism when, to her horror as a chaste maiden lady, he mistakes her for his long-lost mother.

Film writer Paul Dehn had the last word when he said: "It preserved six succulent performances, as though in aspic, for posterity, including Miss Margaret Rutherford's Miss Prism, just sufficiently in control of her romantic longings to snap them back into their proper place as cleanly as she snaps the pince-nez back to her bosom."

With Stringer she then went to France for special scenes together in *Innocents in Paris*. Her own fame had grown by leaps and bounds, leaving him far behind, so that somewhat guiltily she now insisted in all her contracts that her husband be given at least a small role; in this picture it was a good one.

They had decided that Paris would be the scene of their real-life second honeymoon as they left an England that was still recovering from the war. They were both amazed to see an abundance of food in the French restaurants.

"So much farmhouse butter!" exclaimed a delighted Margaret.

Stringer played a rather eccentric British artist mystically linked to the Mona Lisa, which painting in the Louvre he had faithfully copied some three hundred times without selling one of them. Margaret was a spinster painter who had just sold her picture of Montmartre to an American millionaire. She then bought one of Stringer's Mona Lisa's. There was even a suggestion of romance between the two middle-aged artists.

They had a lovely time in France like the two happy children they always seemed to be on such occasions. Tony de Grunwald never forgot Margaret's first visit to the Eiffel Tower, when she announced in a loud voice: "Oh, I had no idea it was openwork."

So excited were Mr. and Mrs. Davis on their first visit to the Louvre that, still wearing heavy movie makeup, they dashed hand-in-hand upstairs to the galleries.

Margaret had always believed in *real* ghosts. "Either one takes them seriously or not at all," she said. So they loved their first visit to the famed gardens at Versailles, where Margaret experienced "a strange ethereal feeling of being transported back in time." This was a source of great personal satisfaction to her, for she had just read a book about the Versailles ghosts that made them sound, in her own words, "commercially vulgar." "Even respectable ghosts have a certain continued right to their privacy," she remarked to an astonished guide in word perfect French.

Some time later, while being driven by a very efficient woman author to a fête in Essex, England, the subject of this same ghost-defaming book came up. Margaret and Stringer both voiced their anger and said just how much it had upset them. Little did they then know that their driver had written it!

Elfrida Down Kettleborough recalls Margaret's loyalty to old friends in such a busy year as this. "In 1952," she told me, "I was asked to help Stephanie Mullins nurse Miss Margaret Mullins, former headmistress of Raven's Croft where Margaret herself had been a student. She had suffered a stroke and some change of personality, and old girls and old friends tended to fall off in their enquiries during her long illness. Peggy was made of different stuff. She never failed to ring and ask affectionately after Miss Mullins. This was at a time when she was in great demand as an actress. I always respected her for this and her love and care for our mutual friend."

My mother and father were both at the hospital bedside when Elizabeth Orphin died. She managed to hold both their hands and given them her seal of blessing. At last her beloved Missy had a man to take care of her; Elizabeth could die content.

Mother had one of her visions:

> We knew that she would not recover and as she turned her face towards the light her breath came in small gasps, and strangely it seemed as if a strong breeze had entered the room and was fanning her face. In that moment I saw Elizabeth as she must have looked as a young girl striding across the heath with her hair blowing in the wind. She had a triumphant look in her face as she sank back into the pillows and slipped away.

She bequeathed her insurance money to her Missy. It was all that she had to leave.

Stringer and Margaret were also at Janie's bedside when she died in Highgate Hospital. "She was my first dresser and she will be there in spirit as my last," Margaret said. Another Cockney, as a child she had danced to the tune of a barrel organ in the streets. Then she had run off to America where she became a bareback rider in a circus. Mother never surrounded herself with uninteresting people.

Janie was able to read her favorite detective stories and all the murders in the *News of the World* right up until the day she died, when "she began to have visions of heaven." Propped up on her pillows, she demanded of a rather startled Stringer: "Can't you see how beautiful it is? They are coming in their chariot to get me." Then raising her hands as if in blessing, she too passed away.

For the rest of her life, whenever she "moved into a new play," Mother always stood a photograph of Janie, dressed in her best Sunday serge, in the center of her makeup table.

There was a ghost in *Castle in the Air,* a movie that Margaret needed little inducement to make, for with kilt, cloak, and beret she felt very much at home. Among her fellow guests she discovers the man she believes to be the rightful king of Scotland. She refused to have a stand-in blow the horn to call in the clans to introduce them to her exciting new discovery. She had never blown a Scottish horn before and it needed an awful lot of wind to do so, but being Margaret Rutherford, she soon learned. It was all a bit hard on Stringer's ears, so he and Minnie the stuffed mouse were dispatched for a walk on their own while Margaret stayed behind and practiced.

By the time the film was completed, she could honestly boast: "I felt every inch a Scottish woman and even switched my evening cocktail to a little whisky in order to get just the right atmosphere."

In *Curtain Up,* based on the comedy *On Monday Next,* Margaret shared acting honors with her old friend Robert Morley. Robert played the producer of a provincial repertory theater whose biggest problem was Margaret playing Catherine, the temperamental and annoying amateur author. It was only a wisp of a part but it did increase her prestige in America. The *American Star* noted: "This film will be greeted with wild enthusiasm by the growing membership of the Margaret Rutherford cult." The art-type movie houses were even beginning to hold week-long festivals of her films.

Then in 1953 came what she always called "my most satisfying and favorite stage part," that of Lady Wishfort in William Congreve's Restoration comedy *The Way of the World,* directed by John Gielgud, at the Lyric Theatre, Hammersmith.

Eric Keown said:

> In general the critics agree that by the strictest standards
> this production was faintly unsatisfactory. Top marks go to
> Miss Margaret Rutherford, most happily cast as Lady
> Wishfort, whom she plays with enormous gusto in the
> grand manner, waving her jaw menacingly at her enemies
> and behaving like a splendidly padded windmill; very
> funny, and curiously touching.

However, the other critics were divided on the performances of both Margaret and Pamela Brown, who played
Millamant to Gielgud's Mirabell.

The *Times* critic said that Margaret

> resembled a Tenniel drawing of the Red Queen repeated
> in delectable sugar candy, and the Queen seems rather
> surprised to find herself speaking such vigorous Billings-
> gate. But Miss Margaret Rutherford gets in her own sur-
> prising and characteristic way a great deal from the part,
> and everyone enjoys her, especially in her final scene.

T. C. Worsley was not so kind. He lavished his praise on
Pamela Brown, complaining that "Miss Margaret Rutherford
cannot get that formidable jaw of hers round half of Congreve's phases. Comic business is not enough here. She is
drowned in a welter of unprojected sentences. She goes
down with all guns firing; but she goes down."

This was offset by fellow critic Harold Hobson's observation of Margaret's Lady Wishfort.

> In her raddled, vain, man-hunting Lady Wishfort's most
> farcical and absurd rhetoric can be heard the echo of the
> authentic music of her vanished and betrayed romantic
> youth; there is something disturbingly sad, as well as up-
> roariously funny, in this beauty become scarecrow. This is
> a Lady Wishfort who, slightly eccentric, might easily be
> encountered in St. James Park. Yet if one met her by moon-
> light, gliding round the corner of a broken staircase in a

ruined castle, one would be startled, but not surprised. Here is a performance that satisfies the eye by its picturesqueness, the ear by the impeccable musical control that underlies its apparent blustering, and that moves the imagination.

As Keown notes, and so rightly:

> Disturbingly sad, as well as uproariously funny; the phrase pinpoints the rare quality to be found in all but her lightest work. Even then there may be an unexpected moment of expressive quiet, a look in the eye, a little tremble in the lip or the voice to warn us that farce may have a crueller side.

These reviews pleased Margaret, who commented: "In all my work I have tried to give an added dimension to comedy, just as Charles Chaplin in his own way does."

Eternally loyal, when John Gielgud told her some years later that he felt she was rightly cast for her role in *The Way of the World* but that he and Pamela Brown were not, she replied: "I do not agree. On the whole the critics were, I thought, a little unkind."

Margaret and Stringer were now living on the first floor of historic Old Hall in Highgate, a William-and-Mary period mansion where Francis Bacon, statesman, philosopher and "master of the English tongue" had died in 1626.* With its paved walk, scrolled iron gates, and beautiful standard roses it really deserved the title "one of Britain's stately homes." There was a large lawn for Margaret's long striped deck chair, while a spectacular view of the lights of London could be seen from the balustrade at night.

* "Bacon, Francis . . . His cynicism masked a deep sense of insecurity. He was often acutely depressed, and, when, under pressure, he suffered fits of nervous prostration." Howells & Osborn: Bowen, C. D. *Francis Bacon: The Temper of a Man* (London: Hamish Hamilton, 1963).

Well-known author Rumer Godden and her husband, James, lived on the main floor of Old Hall, from where a staircase rose up to Margaret and Stringer's flat. It was to be a momentous time in all their lives. "Margaret Rutherford was one of the people I really and truly loved," says Rumer in a tape she prepared especially for me from her present home in Scotland, "though we didn't meet until we were both fairly far on in life."

In turn, Margaret said of Rumer: "She is my friendly saint. I understand her industry, for in the world of the arts we all need to be disciplined. . . . I envy her sense of organization in the home. She cares for James so well."

Rumer and Margaret met in circumstances that could have been lifted right out of a Rutherford movie. Says Miss Godden:

> When we moved to Old Hall, knowing that Margaret was so famous and that so many people sought her out, we tried not to be intrusive. We only said, 'Good morning' and smiled. One afternoon when I was working in my study I became aware of Margaret walking up and down outside, obviously in great distress, wringing her hands as she often did on the stage. Her face was puckered with worry.
>
> As last I dared to get up and go out and talk to her. I said: "Miss Rutherford, is there something wrong? Is there anything I can do to help?"
>
> She clasped her hands and said: "My dear, you have lived in India; you *must* know about monkeys," and then added, "You see, I'm having a chimpanzee to tea!"

This couldn't have had happened with anyone else but Margaret and yet, as always, with Margaret there was truth behind it; it wasn't fantasy.

She was taking part in a long series of Norman Wisdom films in which she was supposed to be an eccentric old lady who kept a large number of wild animals, including this chimpanzee, which she had to cuddle and bathe and put to bed.

Quickly Rumer rose to the occasion and sought to reassure her neighbor that indeed she did know a little about monkeys, as her husband had had a pet one when he was a little boy.

"I warned her that the chimpanzee would probably shake hands with her and that she must try not to shrink at the extreme coldness of a monkey's hands."

In due course the chimpanzee arrived to have tea, walking hand-in-hand with its trainer. Says Miss Godden, whom Margaret like a good hostess insisted should join the other guests: "It was a *she,* about three years old, three feet high, and dressed in scarlet rompers with a scarlet hair-ribbon."

Just as Rumer had predicted, the chimpanzee was made to shake hands with Margaret. "It behaved very well," says Miss Godden, "except that every now and again it had to get up and turn somersaults!"

The chimpanzee's tea party was the beginning of a true friendship between actress and author.

At this time Margaret and Stringer were experiencing serious tax troubles. They were never very good with money and when they had it were overly generous. Margaret also considered the gentlemen at the Internal Revenue office to be "rudely unrelenting." She had struggled so hard teaching music to make ends meet with Aunt Bessie, and now that she had a little extra, the tax men wanted to take it away. One morning she got up and announced to a shocked Stringer that she had decided to ask Robert Morley to make her a banner and then to march in protest to the Houses of Parliament. "I am quite prepared to suffer the consequences and go to Holloway Jail."

One can only imagine what might have happened if Mother had descended like Boadicea minus her chariot on a startled House of Commons with Stringer and the scarlet-ribboned lady chimpanzee bringing up the rear. Suffice it to be said that it took a personal telephone call from Winston Churchill himself to stop her.

Nevertheless, as Rumer remembers, a lien had been placed against Margaret's earnings (poor Stringer earned too little, so they did not bother about his), and "the tax people kept a watchful eye on every penny they spent."

> They were allowed to spend very little, to employ no household help, to do no entertaining, to have no drinks—that is, alcoholic beverages—and what perhaps was worst of all, no transportation, except what other people provided.
>
> Others would have wilted, but not Margaret Rutherford. She fought back to make up the arrears, and she wasn't young. Every morning at a quarter to eight or earlier, a car would arrive to take her to Pinewood Studios for the Norman Wisdon pictures, which I don't think she would have done in other circumstances because she was in a long-running play, *Farewell, Farewell Eugene*. It was not a good play but it was a marvelous part for Margaret. She had also to break a principle, and this grieved her, that whatever play or film she was in, Stringer *must* have a small part.
>
> Every evening Stringer would go out with an umbrella to meet her. They wouldn't allow her a car to take her to and from the theatre, but like everyone that Margaret knew, a taxidriver became her friend, volunteering to come up [to Highgate] and fetch and take her back. Whether she made a financial arrangement with him or not I do not know, but I can tell you I have never been in a taxi with Margaret where the driver would accept a fare. She was so universally loved.

Rumer and James would purposely waylay them on their way back up the garden path, then invite them to come inside of their own portion of Old Hall and sit by the fire. "We would ask them to enjoy a little drink," recalled Miss Godden, fondly, "as they would not accept anything like a bottle of wine, for Margaret had great pride and dignity. What I would like to emphasize was her nobility. Never, never did I hear Margaret complain."

Co-starring with Frankie Howard in the film *The Runaway Bus,* Margaret was the comic, well-meaning spinster. Stringer became a very efficient traffic controller, moving little flags around a map. The action took place on an airport but full of suspicious characters and a stolen fortune in gold. Always the anxious, motherly type, Margaret thought that "although Frankie was young and understandably nervous, he did give a very good account of himself."

Then there was *Trouble in Store* with Norman Wisdom. Norman, she soon discovered, was one of those special people who had made his own headlines at London's great Palladium. The Rank Organization had signed him to a film contract and then, because of an unfortunate screen test, he was dropped from the film they had in mind for him to do. So, when he appeared to play opposite Margaret, she found his confidence already on the wane.

"All the motherliness in me came out," she said, "as I quickly set out to make him feel at ease. Soon there was a very real warmth and understanding between us."

They often rehearsed their scenes over a hot cup of tea in her dressing room. Norman's reaction: "I felt I was working with a pal."

Margaret played a lady shoplifter to Norman's shop assistant. Said Virginia Graham in her review: "Miss Margaret Rutherford, shoplifting her way through the store with good humor and politeness. . . . the toy train running up her sleeve is a masterly touch. It is the very essence of sophisticated comedy."

Later Margaret and Norman made *Just My Luck,* in which she was the proud owner of her own racehorse with Norman as the good-natured jockey. It was during the filming of this

that he offered her half of the bacon sandwich he had
brought from home for his breakfast. She called it "pure bliss
with a crispy crackle!"

Then at the Palladium, in a performance to benefit theatrical charities, she was again reunited with Frankie Howard in
a comic sketch called *Homecoming* by Arthur Macrae. It was
about two dear old ladies crossing the English Channel on a
steamer.

Wearing a marvelous scalloped hat with crown attached,
she played the White Queen at the Globe in *Alice Through
the Looking Glass.* Much to her chagrin she was not required
to fly this time. Felicity Douglas wrote the adaptation for the
Princes Theatre. "She had great sensitivity," said Margaret.
"Toby Robertson was the director and made us all feel happily at home."

Keown called Margaret's performance as the White Queen
"a major triumph fluttering with moonbeam futility, and
catching in her voice and eyes a kind of vegetable astonish-
ment."

So in spite of their financial ups and downs, Mr. and Mrs.
Stringer Davis still felt their Highgate days to be "very pro-
ductive."

One wintry afternoon while taking a brisk walk on Hamp-
stead, Heath while Stringer stayed home with a sinus condition, Margaret thought that she recognized a young Canadian concert pianist named Malcolm Troup. In a letter
written me September 29, 1980, Malcolm, now Dr. Troup,
Head of Music at the City University, London, tells the story
of that amusing meeting and its intriguing sequel:

> Our first meeting was most amusing—on the old
> Highgate Road. We stared long and hard at each other as
> we first approached like two survivors from a previous life
> trying to place an elusive memory. A moment or two after

she had passed me, something made me turn around and there she was bearing down upon me with umbrella up-raised, determined that I should not escape. My first thought was "What have I done to provoke this?" and I wondered if she intended to scold me for staring. But no— it was to ask me if we had not met before, whereupon, drawing myself up to my full height and in blissful igno-rance of whom I was addressing (not being a regular the-atre- or cinema-goer at the time), said "Perhaps you were at one of my concerts . . . ?" This must have appeared so unusual to Margaret, putting the boot so completely on the other foot as it were, that she promptly invited me to take tea with her the following afternoon in her house in Highgate Village, which had once belonged to Sir Francis Bacon.

That was the beginning of a long and loving relationship between us which was cemented not only by the Poetry and Music programmes which we did for the Apollo Soci-ety but also by a tour of Norway arranged by a friend of mine, Ruth Plant, who was at that time Hon. Sec. of the Anglo-Norse Society.

Next afternoon Malcolm Troup arrived for tea at the Davis home, which was mercifully normal and without a chimpanzee this time. Stringer was very cordial and of course Malcolm was asked if, after tea, he would kindly play the piano for them.

Says Margaret: "We were most impressed and on the spur of the moment I suggested that we do a recital of music and readings in Norway."

Margaret had been interested in the Scandinavian coun-tries since her acting days with Donald Wolfit and the Ibsen plays; the seed had long been present in her mind to actually perform in one of them. Malcolm was intrigued with the idea and agreed.

Dr. Troup gives this word picture of my mother at the time:

Margaret was one of the most generous and open-hearted souls that it has ever been my lot to encounter. The world appreciated her more for the idiosyncrasies of manner by which she held this greatness of soul in check than for her greatness itself. . . . however she was misjudged or downgraded to merely character parts, she succeeded in lighting up and warming a whole generation.

On December 2, 1953, from his home in Lissenden Gardens, London, Malcolm wrote her:

You cannot imagine how happy I was made by your letter which arrived today. Seldom have I received anything so beautiful nor certainly anything quite so heartening in its effect. Words are for me but poor servants, it is to music that I must turn to express the variety of feelings which came to me upon reading your letter but, in that art, I am now strengthened and inspired by the measure of your kindness and understanding.

She had asked if he would play for some friends on December 13, a date that he accepted, saying he would "know at the same time that you were there listening to me."

He had followed up their plans for the Scandinavian tour, telling her that he had spoken to Ruth Platt that morning.

She was most excited at the idea and promised to ring Angus McNaughton and many others who might be in a position to speed matters. She also spoke of the possibility of appearances at the Anglo-Norse Societies in all the leading cities. Lord Tenner was the last person to do this. But despite the fact of there being plenty of publicity connected with this latter possibility, there is exceedingly little financial gain involved since these institutions operate on a limited budget.

Malcolm suggested they they meet at the Danish Club for tea or cocktails "depending on what time you are free" and asking Ruth Plant, "a very sweet person" to join them.

The next paragraph in his letter bears out the strong psychic forces that were present thoughout my mother's long life: "The amazing fact about all this is that even before I met you, Ruth was trying to arrange some orchestral appearances for me in Oslo, so that I am certain there is some extraordinary pattern of events at work here, something which drew us together for some high purpose."

Malcolm was in Paris toward the end of 1953, writing Margaret again that December 31 to say

> how much my thoughts were with you while I was in Paris and especially now on the eve of a new year do I think of you and hope that you will go on being made as happy as you make those around you by your unfailing kindness of heart. . . . This last year, as I think back over it, has held much for me, not the least of which was my wonderful and so unexpected meeting with yourself.

During the same December, Margaret and Stringer were perfectly cast as the White King and the White Queen in *Alice Through the Looking Glass,* which opened for the holiday season at Her Majesty's Theatre in Brighton. It was a landmark performance for my father and one of the few parts worthy of his own considerable talents as an actor that he was to receive during their marriage.

In February the play opened at the Prince's Theatre in London's West End, with a star-studded cast. Binnie Hale played the Red Queen, Michael Dennison the White Knight, and Griffith Jones a dashingly monocled Red Knight. Walter Crisham, the American dancer, played what Margaret called "the most sublime collection of supporting roles." She particularly liked his "tiger lily" interpretation in which he appeared as an Edwardian lady complete with lorgnette through which "she" looked at Alice and the Giggling Daisies.

Said Margaret: "One of my favorite scenes was when I turned into a woolly sheep and sang Stringer's silly-silly lyric:

'Jam, jam tomorrow and jam yesterday but never jam today!'
to the tune of his favorite 'Eton Boating Song'."

It was a performance of *Alice* that was true to the spirit of
Lewis Carroll, *her* creator. "One can only hope and pray in
this age of stage realism that the sheer magic of Carroll is not
denied our children," Margaret told the press. Like the 1983
production of *Alice in Wonderland* in New York, starring Eva
Le Gallienne, eighty-three, as the White Queen, Margaret's
portrayal was also true to the original book illustration by Sir
John Tenniel.

The "great friendship" with Malcolm Troup continued and
the Norwegian tour took place during the following early
spring of 1954. A London *Daily Mail* photograph showing
Margaret at the airport en route was appropriately captioned:
"Only one woman can dress so nonchalantly and get away
with it. Only one woman can knot a scarf so jauntily, button a
cardigan so carelessly, clasp a handbag so ineffectively."

For this one special occasion she had her shoulder-length
hair cut and waved into rather a boyish bob look, set off with
large star-shaped earrings.

Stringer went along too, always a little in the background,
bustling around like a mother hen to see that none of their
several brown-paper carrier bags, filled with such necessities
of life as teapots and egg-cozies, was missing.

The Rutherford-Troup program opened with readings
from Spencer and Shakespeare, progressing to her beloved
Edward Lear (*The Owl and the Pussy Cat*) and other modern
poets. Malcolm's background music and appropriate inter-
ludes were, as she said, "played from the heart and particularly touching." Both reader and pianist found their joint
performances "a heartwarming experience" according to
Margaret. "The audiences were informed and appreciative,
coming on stage and introducing themselves afterwards."
Margaret even found time in the busy schedule to visit a

school in Oslo and read her favorite poems to the English class.

The tour completed, Margaret and Stringer then went on to Denmark alone, where on April 2, 1954, she became the first woman ever chosen to read birthday selections of Hans Christian Andersen's immortal fairy tales. (Michael Redgrave had read them the previous year.) They were guests of the City of Copenhagen, where this special program was organized each year by the national Travel Association of Denmark, the newspaper *Ekstrabladet,* and the Danish State Radio.

For the one hundred forty-ninth anniversary of Andersen's birth, Margaret's co-star was Winston Churchill, whose special message was read by Sir Eric Berthoud, the British Ambassador.

Rumer Godden was also involved in the Norwegian and Danish programs, which was no easy task, for as she says, "Margaret was in dire need of direction where the choice of poems and selections were concerned." This was because Stringer loved "light and delicious lyrics, so because of her love for him, and respecting his taste in verse, Margaret sometimes thought with her heart instead of her head."

Miss Godden explains further:

> Like a great many of us, Margaret always wanted to do what she couldn't. What she was not really good at, and that was not comedy, but serious, almost tragic plays [Sir Donald Wolfit, of course, disagreed]. Her lifelong ambition was to play Elizabeth Fry, and when it come to poetry she was even more difficult. Margaret had little idea of real poetry—though to hear her read *The Lady of Shalott* or in particular *Mrs. Malone* was a very moving experience; but she would ruin a program because she wanted every poem to be beautiful. I remember having to arrange the program for the Hans Christian Andersen Anniversary which she read. Could I make Margaret do the crisp, ironic, humor-

ous Hans Andersen? . . . I had great difficulty in persuading her to do them, such as 'The Scissors and the Shirt Collar.' She only wanted to do the beautiful.

Margaret herself explained why she treasured Eleanor Farjeon's poem "Mrs. Malone":

> It is so beautiful that it is almost unbearable. Mrs. Malone is a little Irish woman who lives all by herself with virtually no money, but she does have enough to produce crumbs for the birds and saucers of food for the stray animals. Eventually when she dies the birds and animals are the only ones who really care. I always tell my Tuft that when he goes to Heaven all the birds from Gerrards Cross will be there to meet him, just like Mrs. Malone.

In Denmark, just as in her native Britain, she was up early as usual, making a dawn pilgrimage to the tiny beamed cottage in Odense where the most popular writer of fairy tales was born, to "commune with his rich spirit." Then she trotted on, with Stringer bringing up the rear, to the nearby churchyard where he is buried.

"I felt Hans to be very close to me on that loveliest of spring mornings," she said, "but then of course we have always been close to one another, for are we not kindred spirits?"

Later she sat in Andersen's own chair while she appeared on television reading in English his "Little Ida's Flowers" and "The Darning Needle," her favorites. Close by were his fuzzy top-hat, traveling trunk, books, very large boots, and the coil of escape rope that he took everywhere. Said Margaret: "There was a quality of pathos and even disillusionment in his work."

She was careful not to offend the friendly Danes, whom she was told had been rather upset by her own good friend, Danny Kaye, who, on a previous occasion, had obliged the press photographers by lying down in Andersen's bed wearing his top hat and clowning with his antique umbrella. Danny had been hurt that unwittingly he had upset his genial hosts by simply being too obliging.

Margaret and Stringer went by ferryboat to Odense, a trip they both enjoyed immensely. On arrival Margaret was presented with two groups of Royal Copenhagen procelain, "The Boy with a Goat" and "The Emperor's New Clothes," both representative of Andersen's fairy tales. They were later placed somewhat precariously (at least so it seemed to me) on top of Stringer's piano, where at times they literally danced as he played "The Eton Boating Song"! She was also the recipient of a set of dolls dressed in Danish national costume, which were given, according to Stringer, "pride of place in Mama's black ebony china cabinet." He later gave them to my daughter, his granddaughter, Natasha Manigault, for a christening present.

In Copenhagen Margaret was the guest of honor when the Royal Danish Theatre celebrated its fiftieth anniversary. Later, at the Danish Embassy in London, the Ambassador presented her with the *Ingenio et Arti,* a gold medal given to artistic people of outstanding merit.

When asked what they had most enjoyed in Denmark, Stringer stepped forward and said: "Feeding the birds at Odense."

Back home in England, the friendship with Malcolm Troup continued. Margaret arranged for him to do some work in the film *Mad about Men,* which she was making at Pinewood Studios. Recalls Malcolm: "And this, with our early morning starts (we lived in close proximity) and champagne breakfasts, was an unforgettable experience for the young man that I then was."

Always generous with gifts when she had the money and with her own possessions when she hadn't, she overwhelmed the pianist with her generosity.

This happy incident in both their lives and its subsequent ending is best told by Dr. Troup:

> When I bought my first house in Islington, a furniture van drew up outside the first day crammed full of beautiful furniture, china, silver and curtains from her Regents Park house for me to use in doing up the house until I could gather together things of my own. All this was afterwards given back. . . . Together we opened local exhibitions and fêtes—I can't tell you how closely our lives became for some years. When she began to speak of our running away together, I realized that despite her maturity she still harboured the emotions of a young girl and that, all unawares, I had probably encouraged her to think that our relationship could become even more intimate. Or again, it may not have been as serious as I then believed and simply have constituted a relief from the tension of theatre-life. Whatever the case, I felt it would be better to curtail our meetings, a feeling which I seem to remember that Stringer also shared. Shortly afterwards I left on an extensive tour and Margaret entered hospital for treatment. We were never to meet again.

Malcolm was right. My mother *did* have the emotions of a young girl. She was really quite ageless and because of this we loved her all the more.

"Nothing about an Anouilh play is easy," Margaret admitted. "It taxes every piece of nervous energy and concentration that you can muster up."

In December 1954 she opened at the Lyric, Hammersmith, in the Patricia Moyes adaptation of Anouilh's *Time Remembered*. Among the Hammersmith first-nighters were two gentlemen who were never to miss future opening nights. They were the theater-historians Joe Mitchenson and Raymond Mander. They saw her play an old French aristocrat, the Duchess of Pont-au-Bronc; her co-stars were Paul

Scofield and Mary Ure. "I am always amazed at Paul Scofield's range as an actor," she said. "He has that rare quality that many actors strive to attain and never do." She always considered Scofield a dear friend.

For the first time during her acting career, Margaret carried a gun. Wearing loud tweeds and a hat surmounted by an overly large pheasant's tail, she went a-hunting in the park. Director William Chappell allowed her to perform her own little concoction of a dance. "It became the highlight of my evening for I once had harbored a secret ambition to be a ballet dancer."

Of her performance, Keown exclaimed: "I cannot think of any other actress who could have fitted this moonstruck fairy godmother so perfectly for Anouilh's artificial Cloud-Cuckoo-Land. It was a part that taxed all Margaret Rutherford's gifts, and to me its performance ranks among her best."

Margaret, as in real-life, never lost her sense of innocence, even when she told Mary Ure: "If you were my daughter—but I have no daughter; I could never have a child. Was it poor Gaston's fault or mine? I never knew. And when he died, it was too late for me to find out."

In April of 1955 the production was transferred to London's New Theatre. Margaret continued to be impressed by Paul Scofield's performance, vowing that one day they would give poetry readings together.

When the play was given in Edinburgh, the Lord Provost insisted that a certain passage be deleted in case it offended the Queen who planned to attend a performance. Snapped Margaret: "Another amputation. It is as silly as the mermaid's tail. How officialdom constantly underestimates the intelligence and humor of our Royal Family."

Later Margaret appeared on television in the same play. She called the new experience "a medium which I found most restricting." Stringer found himself cast as a butler for this special performance. "It is a part he does with great style," Margaret commiserated.

Said Stringer somewhat wistfully: "I get so tired of playing perfect butlers and dotty clergymen."

Lionel Harris directed the television version of *Time Remembered*. The *Wolverhampton Express and Star*'s critic seem to have shared Margaret's opinion: "Eccentricity is Margaret Rutherford's forte, but her ebullient characterisations belong to the stage or the wide cinema screen, not to the narrow confines of the television screen."

On January 17, 1954, Sir Ernest John Pickstone Benn, 2nd Baronet, eldest son of that same kindly Sir John Williams Benn who had spoken up for Margaret's unhappy father, died. He had been born in 1875 at Hackney, Middlesex, and had led a remarkable life. While Sir John pursued his political interests, Ernest as a young man assumed management of the family publishing business, Ernest Benn, Ltd. Their Sixpenny Library and Sixpenny Poets were among the first popular paperback series.

Sir Ernest, brother of Margaret's beloved Aunt Rene (Irene Craig), held strong individualistic views as expressed in his own works, including *The Confessions of a Capitalist* (1925), "Governed to Death" (pamphlet), 1948, and *The State of the Enemy,* 1953. "He was our patriarch," Margaret proudly said at his passing.

Timothy Benn, a director of Benn Brothers, Ltd., as the publishing firm is now known, says:

> My grandfather, Sir Ernest Benn, long took a keen interest in Margaret's career, evidently not allowing the previous generation's differences to interfere with his friendship for his cousin. My father and uncle remember Margaret Rutherford, then an unknown elocution mistress, reading poetry and prose to an invited audience at

Sir Ernest's home, Blunt House, Oxted, in the 1920s. Also
going with a family party to John Gielgud's spectacular
production of *The Importance of Being Earnest* in the 1930s,
when she was first acclaimed as a great star in her own
right, for her performance of Miss Prism.

Sir Ernest and Lady Benn were regular attendants at all
London productions starring Margaret from then on, a tradition carried on by Lady Benn after her husband's death. She
was particularly fond of arranging the kind of family parties
that they all loved at Oxted, with Margaret and Stringer often
the guests of honor. The family realized that Stringer, in
spite of the difference in their ages, was the perfect husband
for their Peggy.

In 1954 Margaret managed to make two films (in addition
to her stage work), one of which, *Aunt Clara,* directed by
Anthony Kimmins, was a favorite of hers. Ken Wlaschin,
program director of the London Film Festival and an editor
of the *National Film Theatre Magazine,* described Margaret
as "a nice little old lady who inherits a brothel."

Playing a social worker given to floral-covered straw bon-
nets and enormous white lace collars, she wakes one morning
to find she is the sole heiress in an aged swindler's will. In
addition to his private brothel, which was bad enough, she is
bequeathed his doped greyhounds, gambling booth, and
short-measure pub. With true Rutherford energy and a grim
sense of resignation, Margaret sets about to cope with and
to remedy the strange situation in which fate has placed
her.

Tongue-in-cheek, Stringer this time played the doctor,
which in itself was something of a challenge as in real life
he often joked of "my utter inability to locate my own
pulse."

Henry Markin was Margaret's co-star. "He has such
wicked eyes," she said.

Then she repeated her role as Nurse Carey in the second Miranda film, *Mad About Men,* with Glynis Johns again cast as the mermaid. Stringer was the astonished English vicar who finds genuine antique gold doubloons in his Sunday morning collection plate.

Margaret enjoyed eating Miranda's real pork sausages ("they kept up my strength"). Her patient, of course, only ate fish.

With scorn Margaret declined director Ralph Thomas's offer to supply a double for her fully-clothed diving scene. Her early morning swims in frigid Highgate Pond had not been in vain. Afterwards the studio staff applauded vigorously when Nurse Carey, starched uniform dripping and covered with green slime, was helped out of the water.

In 1955, under J. Lee Thompson's sympathetic direction, she played Prudence Croquet, the owner of a pet store in the memorable picture *An Alligator Named Daisy,* adapted from the humorous book by Charles Terrot. During the filming Margaret became quite attached to her reptilian co-star. "She used to let me feel her heartbeat and I swear that she would smile back at me."

She would have liked to have taken Daisy home for the weekend but Stringer firmly (if gently) put his foot down.

"An alligator might be a little distracting to the neighbors," he said.

In spite of her busy schedule both in the theater and at the picture studios, Margaret always found time for poetry. "I enjoy listening to poetry only slightly less than reading it, as I have done in St. Paul's Cathedral, in the new Coventry Cathedral, at London's Apollo Society, and on the radio," she said.

With Stringer, she believed that John Carroll, who was to give such joy to their declining years and who became an intimate part of the Rutherford-Davis *special family,* "had done more to preserve living poetry" than anyone else. As Margaret explained: "He has taken it off the bookshelf and given it a three-dimensional quality."

She often attended the readings that John arranged, where she cut a memorable figure in her long green cape and silver bracelets. Lady Antonia Fraser, wife of playwright Harold Pinter and herself the biographer of Mary Queen of Scots and Cromwell, wrote me: "I often saw your mother at the poetry readings in the National Portrait Gallery . . . and *how* she loved them."

Of Margaret's own skills as a reader of poetry, fellow actress Joyce Grenfell, the enthusiastic gym mistress of *Happiest Days of Your Life,* says in her autobiography: "Margaret Rutherford read poetry better than almost anyone I ever heard, even better than she played those endearing caricatures she was so justly famed for."

John Carroll, Paul Scofield and Joy Scofield, Paul's wife, accompanied Margaret to have tea with poet Walter de la Mare in his flat, which Margaret, with her keen sense of history, noted "was in one of the last surviving rows of Georgian houses in Twickenham." Margaret, who considered teatime "a very civilized occasion" and remembered Stringer's maxim, "some of the most important questions in life have been settled at the teatable," was enchanted by the aging de la Mare.

The guests had been invited to discuss a special poetry reading that Paul planned to do with Margaret, which program John had been asked to compile. It was to be the first in a monthly series at the Mercury Theatre.

Margaret was enjoying a collection of antique silver tea caddies that had belonged to Queen Charlotte, consort of King George III, when the distinguished poet quietly came into the room.

Noting that "his keen eyes appraised me," she described

their host: "He was a small, striking-looking man; he had a fine aquiline nose and a cap of gray hair."

Later even though it was a raw, cold November day, he introduced her personally to his favorite plane tree in the garden overlooking the Thames.

Said Walter de la Mare to my mother: "It's a friendly tree and my guardian angel. Surely a living tree like that must have some kind of soul?"

"Of course it has a soul," affirmed Mother.

Yet with such an interesting and diverse life, Mother was still plagued with the fear that one day she might go insane like her father.

"My nerves aren't the best," she told Howard Thompson of *The New York Times*. "I've had two breakdowns. Work can be a cure, but psychiatry saved me. I'm religious in that I believe in individual destiny guided by Providence, the All-Powerful. There is this strength from which we draw our own strength."

Margaret Rutherford spoke with honesty and candor about her mental problems. While Stringer "mothered" and protected her throughout these unfortunate spells, he did not like to discuss them. There was a certain stigma, he thought, to mental sickness.

In a BBC interview with Alex McIntosh, Margaret confessed: "One only has a breakdown when one feels that the whole of one's object for living has gone. One has lost one's roots, one has lost one's bearings; that, I think, is almost the deepest sadness that can be imagined in the world today and it is for that, that I have the most compassion, for people who are in that state, I think because I have been in that state myself."

McIntosh then said: "The reason I ask this, Miss Rutherford, is because one never expects somehow a funny person to become ill. We hope that they will make us laugh; we never expect them to be sad."

She almost interrupted him in her eagerness to reply. "Oh, but surely you realize that you never have a comedian who hasn't got a very deep strain of sadness within his or her nature. One thing is incidental on the other. Every great clown has been very near to tragedy, you know; comedy springs from it, I think."

"Which leaves me to ask," said McIntosh, "how far do you allow yourself, Margaret Rutherford, to go along with you in a part?"

Margaret's answer was spontaneous: "I turn her out at once if ever I see her anywhere but then I don't always know when she is about, you see." McIntosh laughed aloud as she continued: "But my great delight in being an actress is to escape, turn myself into some other person."

She was happily married and had the most understanding and doting of husbands, yet even he could not fully protect her from the great strain of living two lives at the same time, her own and the usually eccentric character she was playing. In her autobiography she explains: "All through my acting career I have suffered from overstrain and breakdowns. It is not the least uncommon in the theatre world where we actors walk a tightrope between nervous and physical exhaustion and live in a mixed world of fantasy and reality."

She was not the only actress to suffer from what she termed "my melancholia." For some a change of role worked wonders, but for Margaret Rutherford, rest in a nursing home was necessary. There, with Stringer as her only visitor and surrounded by his posies of wildflowers and the get-well cards he had so carefully chosen, she would gradually find herself.

After one such breakdown in 1956, she was recuperating in a favorite guesthouse overlooking the South Downs near

Brighton. When Binkie Beaumont wanted her for Gerald Savory's play *A Likely Tale,* Dorothy Mather, Margaret's agent, was advised by Stringer to reply: "Margaret is in one of her nonpersuasive moods at the moment."

Robert Morley, just as jovial as he was on stage, was not one to accept such excuses, and besides he knew the real Margaret too well; like a latter-day Aunt Bessie, he phoned: "Now dear, I'm coming down to see you tomorrow," and he did!

Quite firmly he told her to pack her bags, for he had found her a nice part in a new play. He simply would not take no for an answer. Besides, he had a trump card. Stringer had been offered a role in a theater production of *The Devil's Disciple.*

The sudden interest in Stringer's waning career makes one wonder if, like Margaret, he had not found a fairy godfather too. In any case, Morley's simple strategy worked. Explained Margaret: "He had given up so many good parts over the years to be near me, so everything worked out very well."

Stringer packed her bags and, after promising to look after Margaret, Robert Morley whisked her off to Fairmas, his beautiful period home near Henley-on-Thames where he lived with his wife, Joan, daughter of that immortal actress Dame Gladys Cooper, and their three children.

"They took me in with loving arms. Stringer was now on tour, so I thoroughly enjoyed the experience of being kidnapped."

Robert Morley himself has something to say about being called a kidnapper! Says he:

> Of course, it is simply not true that I kidnapped her just before rehearsals began for *A Likely Tale,* but she had become somewhat disadvantaged by an attack of nerves and decided on a rest cure in, I think, Ramsgate [actually it was near Brighton] at a small nursing home cum hotel to which she banished herself along with her eye shade which

she was wont to don when she felt things were getting on
top of her.

After a rather unsatisfactory tea I told her how happy I
was that she could now afford to retire from our ridiculous
profession and how wise she was to have saved up for such
a luxurious retirement. I don't think that Margaret had
particularly enjoyed the tea and decided there and then
she couldn't afford it at all and I drove her to my home
where she stayed while rehearsing *A Likely Tale.*

The least demanding of guests, she did insist however on
a plate of sandwiches in case she woke in the night. She
always made a little sortie upstairs before her evening
stroll on unlighted country lanes in the pitch dark and
when she returned found another plate in her bedroom.

On the pre-London tour with a free morning she occasionally betook herself to a local head shrinker demanding
a release on medical grounds but the medical profession
were unanimous that the best therapy was to continue to
act, until she managed to discover one at Brighton who
opined she could do with a rest whereupon the management announced they were to bring a law suit against him
and he revised his diagnosis.

In the play she was as usual brilliant. After two years I
decided unwisely to close the piece and try my hand at a
disastrous musical version of *Fanny.* When I asked her if
she would mind if we closed, she replied, "Oh, darling, can
we really stop doing this nonsense?"

Every morning Robert and Margaret drove to London for
rehearsals and then home again in the evening. Margaret,
green cloak flying in the wind, took long solitary walks
through the countryside before going to bed. At first she ate
her meals alone in her room; then, getting to know and love
the Morley family, she felt well enough to join them regularly for dinner. Her confidence returned and she said: "Robert and Joan had achieved the impossible and rescued me
from my melancholia."

Gerald Savory's *A Likely Tale* concerned two elderly sisters, played by Margaret Rutherford and Violet Farebrother. They lived in a great old house in Margaret's own Wimbledon, evoking for her nostalgic memories. Concerning her role as Mirabelle Petersham, a sixtyish spinster, Margaret said: "I wore a bandeau on my head with a rose on one side in a kind of twenties teashop style."

A Likely Tale opened for a twelve-month run at the Globe Theatre in March. The reviews were mixed, but the public liked it.

Eric Keown said that Morley "as a self-centered old pussy cat was splendid. Spinster Margaret still sees her long lost Captain de Vaux even in the young man who comes to value the china."

Anthony Cookman, critic for *The Tatler,* dissected the play as follows:

> What is wrong chiefly with *A Likely Tale* is the author's approach to his subject matter. He cannot make up his mind whether to set autumn leaves stirring gently in a sort of Chekhovian comedy or to scatter them madly in a roaring English farce. His autumn leaves are two old maids, the sad but indomitably skittish Miss Margaret Rutherford and the formidably quarrelsome Miss Violet Farebrother, and their brother played by Mr. Robert Morley as a grossly self-indulgent but rather amiable old fuddy-duddy.

Actually Robert Morley played two roles, the old father who sees fit to leave his money to a rest home for retired racehorses, and the son.

"Thanks to Robert and Joan," Margaret happily reported, "and their splendid family, I was fully recovered, and what was most important, I was enjoying myself."

On one occasion during this production she attended a gala tea party with her genial stand-in, Grace Bridges, and without Stringer to gently remind her, quite forgot the time. When she did eventually arrive by taxi for the evening performance, Robert Morley and her worried dresser, Blanche Wright, were pacing up and down outside the theater.

There was no time for false modesty. Said Margaret: "I was entirely realistic. I put my knickers on rushing down the corridor into the wings."

They were off to Ireland this time for the Dublin Theatre Festival. It was May 11, Margaret's birthday, and everybody including the Station Master joined in the impromptu party given her on the platform before boarding the train taking them to the boat. The theater management gave her a bouquet; the cast, champagne and a birthday cake; while the engine driver personally filled the four shocking-pink hot-water bottles she had brought along to keep her feet warm. "We were like a big happy family off to the seaside," Margaret gleefully said.

Once aboard ship she was the only one who kept awake long enough to watch the sun rise over the Irish Sea. Then she quietly slipped back to the cabin where Stringer, covered with one of her many gay woollen shawls, was blissfully sleeping.

From the moment they arrived, Margaret charmed the Irish press, so that a starstruck young reporter wrote:

> I expected today that I was about to meet Madame Arcati and the Professor of Burgundian History, ebullient, dry biscuit-voiced and fluttery. But no, Miss Rutherford was calm, precise, dignified, charming and courtly, and only in a flash from under her eyelids did we perceive the actress who bounces on and off the screen.

She had not been in Dublin since 1938, when she had appeared in *Spring Meeting* at the Gaity. There were so many nostalgic landmarks to find all over again and this time she had her Tuft to share them, "with the clear, inquisitive eyes of a child with which he sees everything."

115

She had replaced her unique Miss Prism with the aristocratic Lady Bracknell in this Irish production of her old favorite, *The Importance of Being Earnest*. With Michael MacOwan directing, the Olympia Theatre production would be called "impeccably stylish" by the *Irish Times*, "a production that never breaks from its sprightly trot into an unruly gallop."

For Margaret there was special praise: "Many theatregoers will remember most clearly the magnificent Lady Bracknell of Margaret Rutherford, a man-o-war in full sail; this is a comedy performance of great tradition."

When she found that *Juno and the Paycock*, the Irish classic, was playing at the Abbey Theatre close by, Margaret was determined to see it in what she called "its rightful setting." Pulling a coat over her petticoat and still wearing Lady Bracknell's outrageous wig and full makeup, she left during the second act of her own play, and sitting in a box, managed to see at least some of *Juno* with what she so aptly called "its militaristic split-second timing." "Oh, had my life been otherwise, I would have enjoyed studying with this fine Irish company," she said a little wistfully.

The Irish had a wonderful time springing surprise parties on the receptive cast. Regretfully Margaret had to forego the last and best of them "on principle." Said she: "I had arrived at the theatre in slacks, breaking my personal rule that trousers should be worn only in private, and I felt that I simply could not attend the party."

What she most appreciated, while performing at the City Theatre in fabled Limerick, was the young boy who, during the first act, ran home "for dear Miss Rutherford's tea made fresh by my Mum." It was delivered in due course steaming hot in his mother's best pink and gold teapot covered by an appropriate green cosy.

Of her hosts, Margaret had this to say: "How I enjoyed the warm informality of the Irish. They really know how to live!"

Lord Wakehurst, then Governor of Northern Ireland, invited the entire cast to an official garden party while they were playing in Belfast. Margaret wore what she describes as "a cloud of blue nylon chiffon with a confection of pink and blue cornflowers on my head." As her bad corn was hurting more than usual, Stringer stitched artificial daisies across the comfortable new sandals that she had to wear. Said Mother: "I felt like a multicolored Orpington hen with her brood of chicks trailing after her."

(I asked Aunty Babs, who used to live near Orpington, the definition of an Orpington hen, but she didn't know either!)

Back in Liverpool at last, Mr. and Mrs. Stringer Davis hired a bus so that the entire company could travel to Edinburgh "like a family, and not segregated in First and Third class compartments as they would have been by train." "Besides," said Margaret, "Many of my best contacts have been made on buses, and I am terribly attached to the dear things."

She also explained their extravagance in hiring the bus: "It was June the Fourth and Tuft's birthday. I just had not had the time to go out and buy him a present." She asked the astonished driver, who was also invited, to "kindly stop your vehicle at the best hotel in Dumfries for a champagne birthday luncheon."

Said the driver: "Thank you kindly, Mum, but may I have a beer instead?"

Off again to Edinburgh, she again ordered her hired bus to stop so that Stringer could feed some obliging sheep. One forward ewe promptly butted his bottom.

Again the tour was a great success, although toward the end some of the cast were "feeling rather off color." Margaret decided that Aunt Bessie's cure for everything, straight cod-liver oil, was the answer, and with Miss Rutherford holding the spoon, nobody, including Stringer, dared refuse her.

During this happy time, the delightful Damaris Hayman was Margaret's understudy. She became particularly dear to both the star and her husband, so that in private life she was invited to become part of their special family. She was always on hand when Margaret needed her, including the time that Margaret dived into the deep end of an icy swimming pool "to tone up my muscles" with such ferocity that she broke both of her shoulder straps.

"I came up thrashing about and blowing water like a friendly walrus until Damaris gallantly swam with two safety pins in her mouth to aid me."

In Edinburgh a grateful fan presented Margaret with "a beautiful potted plant with some elaborate South American name sitting in a wicker basket." Damaris was delegated to be its nurse, carrying it on the bus in her lap "like a mother-less child" and watering it regularly in the ladies' powder room. It was also Damaris who selected the antique green Bristol glass whisky decanter at Ernest Pickering's antique shop in Eastbourne for the company's parting gift to Margaret and Stringer.

Mother loved to give that green decanter a wicked little look but, then say with a chuckle: "The cast thought this to be the most appropriate gift, seeing all the drinks that we had given them."

In September of that same year, 1957, Margaret and Stringer began a successful tour at the invitation of the Aus-trialian Elizabethan Trust. They broke their long air journey to Australia in Beirut and again in Singapore. In addition to inspecting the Baalbec ruins and the American College in Beirut (they were equally impressed with both), they went on a shopping spree; free at last of the taxman's restraint, Margaret having worked off all that was owing, they com-pletely overspent themselves. "Can you imagine me set free in an Arabian bazaar?" Mother was to ask me. "Dear heart, it was as busy and exciting as a harem."

For the rest of their lives they would both sing the praises of the manager of Singapore's Raffles Hotel, who graciously accepted their British check.

On their arrival in Sydney they were warmly welcomed by Hugh Hunt, representing the Elizabethan Theatre Trust. He had been highly recommended by their good friend, Elsie Beyer of H. M. Tennent Ltd., Binkie Beaumont's theatrical enterprise. They had been lent an apartment at Point Piper with a panoramic view of the harbor. There they carefully unpacked their own brown teapot, eggcups, and Aunt Bessie's somewhat moth-holed egg cosies which fitted snuggly over their boiled eggs.

Margaret's Aunt Maysie Nicholson, a resident of Sydney, came to help Stringer out with the housekeeping, a gesture that delighted him. The Winter Garden Cinema was screening *Aunt Clara* in honor of the Rutherford visit.

Said Margaret: "We arrived in Sydney the morning after Elizabeth Taylor and her dear Mike Todd had thrown one of their parties, but the press manfully and womanfully gathered to welcome us." She was particularly impressed with Andrea of the publication, *Truth.* "She was polite and yet honestly outspoken, qualities that I admire greatly."

The tour opened in Sydney with John Dighton's *The Happiest Days of Your Life,* which they were to repeat in Tasmania in a very warm January, and later take to Melbourne. The friendly Australians gave Margaret Rutherford a warm response and have never forgotten her. Margaret, however, was particularly happy with the Sydney *Daily Mail's* headline: THEY DON'T CALL HIM MR. RUTHERFORD. The piece began: "The background in sixty-five-year-old Margaret Rutherford's life is her marriage partner, and he is *no* silent partner." This pleased Margaret because Stringer was so often forgotten by the press, except when he was writing stimulating letters to the London *Daily Mirror* or later sticking up for me in the only newspaper that would listen to him, the London *Daily Telegraph.* As to the Australian compliment,

Mrs. Davis declared: "Stringer has been, and always will be, a fine actor in his own right as well as being a remarkable husband."

Again they went shopping together but he did put his foot down when she wanted to buy him a large plaque of the Sydney Harbor Bridge. "But darling, the bridge girders are not in the right place," he countered. Later he appeased her hurt feelings with his own personal gift of a bone china blue-bird in a little golden cage. In return she gave him a tiepin shaped like a boomerang.

Douglas and Dorothy Dundas planned Margaret's reading at the National Gallery to such a full house that she was asked to give a repeat performance the next evening. Wilson Hogg arranged a further reading at the Trinity Grammer School, and there was yet another at the Geelong Art Gallery. Grace Stafford and Sam Dempsey of the local education department invited them to hear a hall full of schoolchildren, aged from eight to twelve years, read and recite poetry. Enraptured young faces then listened as Margaret repeated the gesture.

New friends were made everywhere; she was over-whelmed by the genuine adoration shown her by the Australians . . . and she was at her endearing best. Stringer would forget himself and shout "Isn't she terrific" as his wife walked proudly like a queen among the crowd.

She once received an Aborigine boy from the Northern Territory in her dressing room. He had recently won a competition for writing a little play and was in Sydney to hear its first broadcast. He was fascinated with the picture of Janie, the Cockney dresser, sporting her best Sunday serge, and even more so when Margaret carefully explained that Janie had once ridden a horse bareback in a circus.

She also found time to encourage another young visitor, Noel Risby, then sixteen. Said she: "He so longed to be a show business journalist."

The Katoomba Repertory Company invited Margaret and Stringer to visit them in the Blue Mountains, where a councillor greeted them on behalf of the mayor, who was away fighting a bush fire. Said Margaret: "He had a face like dark brown chamois leather."

She appeared in both *Blithe Spirit* and *The Importance of Being Earnest* for radio, and later "ate far too much cake . . . it had lovely hard pink icing," at a party given her by women university graduates. She also delighted members of the Overseas League with an informal visit.

At Hobart, in addition to acting, she was introduced to "the sympathetic Rowntree sisters" and the poet Clive Sanson, whose work, "The Witness," she had included in one of her recent readings. At Glenelg she met an aunt, Edith Nicholson, who found them "a flat just like Henry Worthing's house in *The Importance of Being Earnest*." When she said that it was "appealing swimming in seaweed," the international press picked up the story. Margaret even sampled the safety of a sharkproof swimming pool.

In Melbourne, where she again played in *Happiest Days,* the cast also rehearsed Jean Anouilh's *Time Remembered* for a special presentation in Adelaide. Before returning to their base in Sydney, Mr. and Mrs. Davis were both presented to Sir William and Lady Slim in their box after the performance. Margaret told Sir William how much they had both appreciated the sincerity of the Australian people. Sir Robert Menzies gave Margaret his impressions of Sir Winston Churchill in World War II, after which she declared that had the great man not chosen to be a statesman, "with such a fine delivery he could always have been an actor." She also mentioned "your fine Australian accent. It is such a pity that some Australians seem ashamed of their natural speaking voices."

Before their ship left Sydney for the long voyage home on June 4, 1958, Margaret gave Stringer a ball to celebrate another birthday. "I felt rather like the Sun King having a ball all to myself," said Father. "All that I lacked was a white satin suit."

Just before they sailed away, Margaret told the press that "the entire tour has been most stimulating," to which Stringer added: "As for me, I would like to live in Sydney more than any other place in the world."

On the way home Mother decided that she could not face the heat of the Suez Canal, so they left the ship in Ceylon (Sri Lanka) and flew the rest of the way to London. Father said that Mother just wanted an excuse to have a third honeymoon in what she called "that most romantic of islands, surrounded by its mysterious gunmetal sea."

Another breakdown, a restful recovery, and then back to work! In 1959 she appeared in *Dazzling Prospect* by John Perry and Molly Keane, whose other play, *Spring Meeting,* had served her so well. Noel Coward was at the opening, finding the play to be "quite disastrous . . . disgracefully directed by Johnny Gielgud." He did concede that "Margaret Rutherford was funny at moments."

The audience booed and the reviews were, as Coward said, "appalling."

On opening night Mother was so downcast that she treated Father to supper at the Savoy.

·7·

Mother Rutherford, O.B.E.

"The time has come," the Walrus said, "to talk of
many things: of shoes and ships and sealing wax, of
cabbages and kings, and why the sea is boiling hot
and whether pigs have wings."

From *Through the Looking Glass*
by Lewis Carroll;
a favorite quotation of Margaret Rutherford

NEVER one to waste valuable time, after reading a humorous bestseller, *Me Papoose Sitter,* Margaret Rutherford sat right down and wrote a letter to me.

"When I read this delicious book I immediately identified
with this old Indian lady, wanting to play her in the film being
planned from its pages," Margaret Rutherford wrote.

The motion picture rights were held by the British actor
Anthony Dawson, who had for a year played the villain's role
in the Broadway version of *Dial M for Murder,* later recreat-
ing his part in the movie version with Ray Milland and Grace
Kelly (the late Princess Grace of Monaco). Margaret wrote
Tony Dawson to know where she could find me. Stringer
remembered later that "we both shared the premonition that
the author was very special; perhaps waiting to fulfill something that had been missing in both our lives."

They were to discover that I was then living in the
Greenwich Village section of New York City with a distant

cousin, Isabel Lydia Whitney, America's first woman fresco painter and a professional watercolorist. Although she liked to say "I am not one of the horsey Whitneys," she was related to John Hay Whitney, then American Ambassador in London, and Gertrude Vanderbilt Whitney, a founder of the Museum of Modern Art. Around the corner from her West Tenth Street home were her close friends, artists Edward and Jo Hopper. They had been young together and kept in close touch every day by telephone.

Isabel was a very private person. A Christian Scientist, she liked to boast that her mother, Martha Hasseltine Whitney, who had marched down Fifth Avenue demanding the right for women to vote, had refused to give "a drawing room" (a fund-raising benefit) for evangelist Billy Sunday (as one of the Vanderbilt women had done) because he had criticized Mary Baker Eddy, founder of Christian Science, and hated suffragettes.

Margaret was determined to meet me and press her case for the role of Poor Old Grandmother in *Me Papoose Sitter*. Finally the opportunity came; in 1960, she arrived in New York with Stringer to play in the Broadway version of *Farewell, Farewell Eugene*.

Hand-in-hand they walked up West Tenth Street until they found Number Twelve with its great black double doors and what Isabel called the Medusa Scrollwork, which resembled the tresses of a woman's hair. Looking up at the fourth-floor windows, which were wide open, Margaret told Stringer: "A Britisher lives there—plenty of fresh air." They rang the doorbell and waited, Margaret later said, "Like two hopeful travelers at the end of a long journey. An ethereal feeling swept over us."

The door was opened by Miss Whitney's combination butler-bodyguard-handyman, a Sicilian named Joseph Scaltro who, as Stringer said, was "very outgoing."

"He greeted us profusely, more like the master of the house than the servant," said Stringer. "He wanted to know if we were hungry, then suggested that we might like a glass of wine, at the same time warning us that the only wine in the house had been left over from Miss Whitney's father's funeral tea in 1932. We were tempted but feared it would be too potent."

Isabel and I had decided to receive Margaret Rutherford and her husband in my sitting room, rather than in Isabel's double drawing room on the second floor, which, with its lavish antiques always seemed to me like the Metropolitan Museum. Tea would be served in my small writing room where Margaret would be asked to sign one of the bookshelves as other famous visitors such as Pearl S. Buck, Frances Parkinson Keyes, Joan Crawford, and Princess Ileana of Romania had already done.

Margaret's description of Isabel and me has survived:

> They could both have stepped out of a play. Miss Whitney, ageless and gracious with her bluish-gray hair piled high upon her head rather like Queen Mary's. It was ironic that she, who in her youth had made national headlines when she had climbed to the top of a skyscraper to paint a fresco, should have crippled herself by falling off of a kitchen chair. She walked with a light aluminium crutch which she manipulated with the dexterity of a nubile mountain goat. . . .
>
> The child [she called me "the child" right from the start of our relationship] was dark haired, high-cheekboned and frail. . . . Gordon's* large brown eyes, inherited from some long-dead Andalusian ancestor, haunted me all through that evening's performance. . . . He sat with a large green and red Amazon parrot named Marilyn on his

---

* "Dawn," after the operation which removed the residual male sexual characteristics with which she had been born.

shoulder. She had just been photographed for LIFE magazine.

Stringer was made somewhat nervous by the solid silver teaballs: "Cannonballs would be the better word," he confessed. "I was afraid of cracking the cup."

During the autographing in the library, Margaret exclaimed like a little girl discovering a new secret. "Oh, the Archbishop of Canterbury . . . Dr. Geoffrey Francis Fisher . . ." She clapped her hands and began to hum William Blake's *Jerusalem*. Isabel quickly explained that we had entertained both the Archbishop and Mrs. Fisher and that I had been invited to dinner with them in Lambeth Palace. They had been very interested in my morality play, *Saraband for a Saint,* which, with its strong interracial theme, had been presented in the chancel of St. Martin's Episcopal Church in Harlem.

Ann Guerin, our pleasant Irish housekeeper, came in with a pile of autograph books for Margaret to sign. Some of Ann's relatives had seen Margaret perform on the recent Irish tour.

Then Isabel asked Margaret if there was anything she would like to do during her stay in America. "I would like to have Thanksgiving" was the prompt reply.

"Well, I think that *could* be arranged," said Isabel, at the same time looking imploringly at her Sicilian bodyguard, who was hovering behind a life-sized cloisonné vase that had been given Isabel's father by the Emperor of Japan. Joseph nodded agreement. He was always game for a good meal and, as he well knew, he would have to cook it. He had chased away the rest of the staff with the exception of Ann Guerin, and had recently taken over the cooking.

"Then that can be easily arranged," said Isabel, quickly changing the subject. "Would you like to go downstairs and see the Botticelli?"

Again Margaret clapped her hands. "I have always wanted to see a real Botticelli angel," she said.

"Then you shall see three," replied Isabel, leading the way on her aluminium crutch down the winding staircase.

As I stood watching them, I felt a strange longing in my heart, a sense of belonging in a real family, something I had never known. There was something about Margaret Rutherford that was easy to define—compassion, understanding, and love. It was all there in her eyes, and when it was time for her to leave with Stringer, she engulfed me in those ample motherly arms.

In spite of the happy Whitney interlude, Margaret and Stringer's second American adventure had encountered difficulties from the start. To begin with, the *Queen Mary* was dockbound at Southampton because of a strike. Reporters asked Margaret if she had brought a cook along, evoking the reply: "I never travel without my favorite," meaning Stringer. "Besides, I am going to be the best waitress the *Queen Mary*'s ever had." The strike continued and, as the rehearsals for the new play were already overdue, they were obliged to take their luggage off the ship and fly to New York instead.

Upon arrival, Margaret told an eager press that they both felt "super-charged." The management had found them a suite at the Hotel Oliver Cromwell, a strange choice for two such ardent royalists. There were windows on all sides affording a splendid view of the city. Seeing all the lights on the first night, Margaret exclaimed: "I am in Fairyland."

The small compact kitchen became Stringer's delight; he never stopped singing its praises for the rest of his life. Carefully he set their favorite Georgian teacaddy, red plastic egg-cups, egg cosies, and teapot on one of the shelves. He still needed a coffee pot and a pressure cooker, which he discovered "on an exciting expedition to the nicest ironmongers on

Columbus Avenue." Their obliging agent, Peter Witt, found them a grill and oven, a must for their nocturnal bacon and eggs "after the theater" suppers. Then the obliging Mr. Witt had a piano moved in, so that tea, accompanied by Stringer's self-composed lyrics, could still be held at four every afternoon.

For an Englishwoman, Margaret would give New York its finest compliment: "Tea in New York is so delicious, much better than in England because the water is purer. So invigorating that it makes us feel like newlyweds. London water is so cloudy and full of disinfectant."

They were visited by Lillian Ross of the *New Yorker,* whose excellent word-picture of the occasion is penetrating and quite to the point. Margaret liked both Miss Ross and what she subsequently wrote about them.

> And to Miss Rutherford we went the other morning, a few days after her arrival, to accompany her to her first rehearsal. We found her, white-haired, gracious, observant, and charming—looking very much the way she did when she played the hearty, bicycle-riding medium in the movie version of *Blithe Spirit*—in an upper–West Side hotel called, of course, the Oliver Cromwell. She was in a three-room, twenty-first-floor, Central Park-view suite that she shares with her husband, Stringer Davis, who is also in the play, and who was also present. White-haired and pink-faced, he was wearing a Harry Truman–type short-sleeved sports shirt that hung loose over the top of his trousers, in the solid American way. Miss Rutherford had on black strap shoes with sensible heels, a blue-green cotton frock, a man's wristwatch on a leather strap, a necklace of Chinese stones, and four rings, two on each hand.

At the theater, Margaret fell in love with her dressing room, "a pink dream with air conditioning." Unfortunately for her, although there was a heat wave in progress, the theater management hadn't turned it on! Finally Margaret had a verbal explosion, demanding that two large electric fans be sent in, "and if you can find it, the large propeller that Joan Crawford had in *Rain*."

Nobody felt like sending to Hollywood for a propeller but Margaret did get her two large fans, which were placed on a table whose other occupants were Minnie the mouse and Flora the orange stuffed kangaroo, (a present from grateful Australian fans, named for actress Flora Robson). Noel the teddy bear had been left to mind their belongings at home.

Upon meeting Mildred Dunnock, one of her co-stars, Margaret was very intrigued with her feet! "So tiny, like an Elizabethan child in a Tudor portrait." She was more conventional in describing Loueen MacGrath: "She has such a lovely sensitive face."

Margaret had agreed to work with a young director, "because," she said, "I find the young so vivid and interesting," but something went wrong between him and the rest of the cast. Even gentle Stringer, who had as usual a small part, became worked up and upset. An enormous row followed, with everybody suggesting his own favorite replacement. "In that case I nominate Stringer," Margaret snapped, causing the rest of the cast to roar with laughter.

Margaret then gathered up Minnie, Flora, and Stringer and returned to the sanity of the Hotel Oliver Cromwell where she promptly took to her bed with a pink rubber hot-water bottle. After some "blasting" phone calls, a phenobarbital tablet, and a large bowl of Stringer's Irish potato soup, she fell "into a long and blissful sleep."

Things finally worked out, including the weather, which mercifully turned cooler. Margaret's New York rehearsal schedule did not allow time for her regular afternoon nap, which, she explained, "recharges the electricity for the rest of the day. Deprived of it I am like a sea lion without its pool."

On Sundays, with Stringer she took the train to Jones Beach "for a swim in the ocean." Even Stringer complained:

"We had to wade knee-deep through Americans reading their gigantic Sunday newspapers before we ever reached the water."

Lillian Ross contributed more information on their Jones Beach adventures:

> "We've been to your Jones Beach and we did get colored up a bit," Miss Rutherford told us.
>
> "My wife is the open-air type," said Mr. Davis. "We took a taxi to the Penn Station, and after a brief exchange with the information gentlemen there we got on the ten-nine and did the change to the bus. At the beach, we hired private rooms, and then went out and landed in those enormous rollers. My wife was bounced about."
>
> "My husband breasted the waves and got beyond them," said Miss Rutherford. "I'm quite a good swimmer, but it was a man-size sea."
>
> "We found the wild hamburger in its lair," Mr. Davis said dreamily.
>
> "Jones Beach is so beautifully *organized*," said Miss Rutherford.

Isabel had planned to wear her father's antique Chinese robe to the opening of *Farewell, Farewell Eugene* at the Helen Hayes but was unable to do so as I had suddenly been taken ill. (The robe had to wait for its theatrical debut until it was worn by my good friend, Carson McCullers when she appeared on Edward Albee's arm for the premiere of *Ballad of the Sad Cafe,* which he had adapted from her book of the same name.)

I was suffering from acute nasal and chest congestion. Isabel did not like having medical doctors come to the house because of her religion. The only way that I could get any sleep at night was to be given a glass of some of the leftover sherry from Mr. Whitney's funeral. Then in desperation, Isabel Whitney called in Margaret Rutherford.

She arrived like some latter-day "Miss Marple" and with

Stringer looking on somewhat nonplussed, she began sniffing around for clues. "Do you have a bad cold?"

"No, Miss Rutherford. I don't usually get colds in the hot weather."

"Did you eat something terrible?"

"No, I usually eat at home. I like simple things."

Then I started to cough and there was no time to hide what I was bringing up . . .

Margaret Rutherford's eyes darted around the room, finally surveying the floor.

"The carpet is also gold . . . interesting."

"I don't see the connection, dear," said Stringer, obviously embarrassed in Isabel's presence.

"Arsenic poisoning," said Margaret, defying us to contradict her. "Don't you remember the story in the *News of the World*? 'Arsenic flakes falling from the ceiling upon Claire Booth Luce . . .' Dear heart, it nearly killed her."

Strange as it may seem, "Miss Marple" was right. The gold carpets that had been given me to use in my suite by Isabel had been for years in storage. They had been liberally dusted with arsenic dust to keep out the moths. In addition, their ancient gold pile had polluted the air.

So on our second encounter, Margaret Rutherford saved my life.

Margaret told us of the "tumultuous applause" of a Broadway first night. Actually, the New York critics adored her personally but did not care for the play.

The most delightful tribute came from Walter Kerr, then critic for the *New York Herald Tribune,* who said that he "had always loved Margaret Rutherford but that by the time she came to America, she had a husband, and he had a wife."

John Chapman in the *New York Daily News* wrote: "There just could not be anybody funnier than Margaret Rutherford, who is a combination of Marie Dressler and a George Price caricature. But there could be a funnier play than the one she appeared in last evening at the Helen Hayes, *Farewell, Farewell Eugene.*

The *New York Times'* Howard Taubman had this to say:

> As the sister who aspires to be rakish she does humorous things with her trembling chin, crinkling nose, and a neatly timed vacant stare. With a shawl over her shoulders and a flower in her hair she does a momentary take-off of Carmen. A pitch helmet adorns her head and she looks like a cartoon of a safari. Munching a slab of salami and draining a beer she is a performer on her own. Who can blame her if she takes care of herself and lets the role go hang?

Poor Margaret could not save the play. "I was heartbroken," she said, "as I quite thought I had let my American public down." Later she was told that tickets had been sold for weeks in advance to women's clubs and other organizations in Connecticut, New Jersey, and New York. "I will never understand American theater producers," she grumbled.

On a happier note, Margaret and Stringer enjoyed an early Thanksgiving with us on West Tenth Street. They also were given a small facet of American history when Isabel related how years before, President Woodrow Wilson, courting, had brought Mrs. Edith Galt, the lady who would be his second wife and one of the country's most remarkable First Ladies, to the Whitney house for another Thanksgiving. The old butler had been most upset as the silver gravy boat could not be found and he had to use an oatmeal bowl instead!

Margaret went back to her suite with a blue milk-glass covered dish in the form of a camel. It was the first of many similar gifts that I was privileged to give her.

What I did not know was that a day or two previously, Margaret and Isabel had met privately to discuss my future. It was then that Isabel had revealed my medical problem.

Robert Carroll, writing in the October 29, 1982, issue of the *New York Daily News* under the heading NOW LITTLE GREGORY IS LITTLE MARJORIE, described a case similar to mine. Doctors determined that the organ thought to be male was instead "an enlarged clitoris."

The baby christened Gregory Jeanty but renamed Marjorie was flown from Haiti to the United States where an operation "reduced the size of the infant's clitoris and enlarged the baby's vagina."

Isabel noted that my voice had never broken and described the hernia that was so troublesome, while Margaret sat like one spellbound. She also told her something that I did not then know, that she was in the first stages of leukemia for which her doctor had told her there was no cure. Financially she would see that I was taken care of; it was the loneliness that she foresaw for me that she dreaded.

A day or so afterward Margaret and Stringer asked me, while on a visit to the Statue of Liberty, if I would like to join their little family. "We would like to adopt from the heart." I was elated, for who would not have wanted Margaret Rutherford for a mother?

The weather had taken a turn for the better but soon they would have to leave. Before departure, with Isabel Whitney looking like a dowager empress in attendance, wearing her mother's "best red lace," and Marie Antoinette's earrings, and the family rubies, Margaret had a gratifying time reading "The Lady of Shalott" and other poetry at the William J. Gaynor Intermediate School. Stringer was rather uneasy. "We needed a bodyguard with Isabel sporting a king's ransom."

Mildred Dunnock invited Margaret and Stringer to visit her country home in Connecticut, which especially pleased Stringer, a great movie buff. Luise Rainer of *The Good Earth* had once lived there.

Hollywood legend Gloria Swanson interviewed Margaret on her weekly radio show, introducing her with the words:

"And here from England is Margaret Rutherford, whom the whole world adores." Margaret's appraisal of Gloria was: "Every inch of that tiny figure is star rating."

Although I phoned Mother Rutherford daily with words of encouragement they were not happy at the prospect, as Father Stringer said, of returning to England "with our tails between our legs." Then out of the blue came a telegram from Danny Kaye inviting my new mother to play a Scottish noblewoman in his forthcoming movie, *On the Double*. Skipping up and down the sidewalk in front of Number Twelve, she exclaimed like a happy child, "Oh, I do hope I can blow the horn again." She then borrowed Isabel's grand piano, upon which Paderewski was once supposed to have played, and Stringer was delegated to compose a musical acceptance telegram that ended with the words: "Oh, blissful day." It certainly was.

For their last evening in New York, Mother and Father gave a rather breezy farewell party. Snowflakes literally blew across the room from the opened windows; some of the women guests were glad of their fur coats.

Isabel disdained taxicabs, calling them a waste of money, although she was a millionaire. As she was wearing the triple diamond necklace her mother had bought from a distressed Russian Princess, I did manage to persuade her that just for this once it would not be prudent to ride to the Hotel Oliver Cromwell on a public service bus.

For once in her life, Margaret Rutherford had keen competition. Cousin Isabel sat in a chair with Margaret and the other guests sitting on the carpet at her feet. It was Margaret who asked her, "Did you know the Roosevelts?" but she was not prepared for the answer.

Said Isabel: "Dad passed away a few days after Mother and I was incensed when my sister and I were expected to pay a double inheritance tax on the same money. So, having been required by a well-meaning aunt to play with Franklin Roosevelt at Hyde Park when we were children, I went to see him at the White House. Politely he informed me that there was nothing he could do. I was furious. 'Franklin,' I said, 'you always were a nasty little boy and you've grown into a mean old man'."

When the party was over, Mother and Father insisted that we stay behind for a real theatrical supper, which turned out to be bacon and eggs. Then, very formally, Father presented Cousin Isabel, who abhorred strong drink, with fifteen bottles of Scotch whisky, left over from the evening's festivities.

Good manners prevailing, Isabel graciously accepted her startling gift. Later we both crept up the brownstone steps to the Medusa doorway each holding a small crate. Looking across to the rectory of the Church of the Ascension, Isabel said, "Pray God that His servant sleeps."

Margaret and Stringer sat holding hands on the plane to Los Angeles. They appeared so blissfully happy that a well-meaning fan on the way to the rest room inquired if "Mr. and Mrs. Rutherford were on a Golden Wedding trip."

As Margaret had requested sea air, Paramount Studios had found them a suite at the Shangri La in Santa Monica. Next morning they sat in the vestibule awaiting the car that was to take them to meet Danny Kaye. The driver who was to pick them up made two trips, returning to the studio the first time with the information that he had not seen anybody waiting "who looked remotely like a movie star."

When they did at last reach Danny Kaye, he greeted Margaret warmly. "How are you, Miss Rutherford?" he said.

"All the better for seeing you, Mr. Kaye," she replied.

"So began a true and gentle friendship," she later wrote. "We developed a sort of armed rapport, each respecting the other's art."

Next morning Mr. and Mrs. Davis were met by an enor-

mous shining Cadillac, in ledgendary Hollywood style. The
uniformed chauffeur was genuinely surprised to find them
waiting for him on the sidewalk with the biggest collection of
paraphernalia he had ever seen: picnic hampers, shawls, suit-
cases, teacaddy, teapot, a carton of eggs, stuffed toys, and
Stringer's precious New York pressure cooker. The Cadillac's trunk was filled to its full capacity and even then, when
Margaret and Stringer were seated at last, there was a further
delay. Margaret had forgotten to pack Janie's portrait, and
sent Stringer back into the Shangri La to get it.

With some relief the patient driver finally got them to
Paramount, where the waiting commissionaire said in a stuffy
voice: "Yes, I have heard of you but do not know if you have
been assigned a dressing room."

The now-embarrassed driver, with what Stringer called "a
look of resignation on his face," unloaded all of their many
belongings on the sidewalk, where like two British orphans
straight out of *Jane Eyre,* the Davises sat cross-legged beside
them, waiting for Danny Kaye to come to the rescue. In due
time, and with many apologies, he appeared.

Margaret was much impressed with the "extreme profes-
sionalism" of making a film in Hollywood. "I have only
happy memories," she later said.

Dancing a Scottish reel with Danny was the highlight of
her working trip. Later, after hiding with him under a banquet table, she said: "Danny was just fooling around, making
fun with me and of me. I felt quite safe for Stringer was never
far away." This time he was playing the butler.

Danny gave Margaret a tea party, complete with a large
Russian samovar borrowed from the props department. Although Margaret was deeply touched, and beautiful Dana
Wynter "expertly worked its organism," she longed to tell
everybody that tea tasted best in a china teapot. "Of course, I
had nothing personal against the Russians; I've always greatly
admired the physical stamina of their Catherine the Great."

For her dressing room she was given "a little house with real street lamps in front, just like Victorian London. I felt quite at home."

The Misfits was being filmed at the same studio and on the last day of shooting, Clark Gable, its star, expressed a desire to meet Margaret. As Stringer was one of his fans, the occasion proved mutually pleasing. Poking his head through her diamond-paned window, Gable said: "Welcome to Hollywood, Miss Rutherford." She never forgot his "surprisingly gentle voice."

Stringer told Clark Gable that he had once met a man of ninety in Glasgow, Scotland, who had boasted of surviving the earthquake in San Francisco.

"I survived it too," said Clark, leaning forward in order to plant a kiss on Miss Rutherford's forehead. Then, turning once under a gaslight, he gave a mischievous smile, waved, and was gone.

Margaret was "overcome" by one of her "psychic feelings." "We knew he was tired," she said, "and that he had had a miserable time on the set, but I suddenly got the impression that he was waving as if he were saying goodbye to films; goodbye, in fact, to everything. And of course, soon afterwards the poor man died."

She also met Marilyn Monroe, calling her "that dear waif-child, whom life and Hollywood were destined to destroy." It was a brief encounter in Margaret's dressing room, during which Marilyn, her blond hair ruffled, played happily with Minnie and Flora. "Then," said my mother, "she lay her sad little face in my lap and was soon asleep."

Margaret and Stringer saw their first color television in Hollywood; they thought the actors' faces "much too red." Stringer did the shopping in the first supermarket he had ever seen. "Lovely, quite lovely," Margaret called the delicacies that he found.

Although she called gourmet cooking "my hobby,"

Stringer did most of the cooking. She had what Stringer called "an affinity for chickens," telling LIFE that his wife was "the finest poultry cook in the world. . . . If I had to have my last poultry dish, I'd certainly want Margaret to cook it."

They enjoyed the Santa Monica beaches where they were photographed doing the backstroke for LIFE, whose photographer took a priceless picture of Margaret kicking up her legs in the water. Hand-in-hand they enjoyed long walks together, during which they made the acquaintance of the statue of "dear little Santa Monica." Wesley Griswald, who befriended them, took them on "magical drives." "Wesley made that extra little difference to our stay in Hollywood," Margaret said.

Before flying home "like two Santa Clauses crossing the North Pole," as Mother wrote me, they sent me a porcelain Meissen monkey. They had signed their names to the handwritten note that read "Thank you for joining our little family."

An ironic family event was to occur on November 17, 1960, when Cousin Tony Benn's father died, automatically making Tony the second Viscount Stansgate of Essex, entitled to sit and vote in that same House of Lords that he had so often said should be abolished!

For ten years Tony had represented Bristol, Southeast, in the House of Commons, the elected seat he was forced to surrender when he became a reluctant aristocrat. Tony wanted no part of the House of Lords; he wished only to return to his beloved Commons. In time he would become the first British peer ever to renounce his title; some three years later he won back his House of Commons seat with an overwhelming majority.

As his American wife, Caroline, told her native *Cincinnati Enquirer:* "He was elected to Parliament to represent a section of the British people. I think that's a much greater honor than inheriting something."

Mother once said rather sadly: "At home I was only to be accepted in my medium as the eccentric lady," so her visit to Malta to appear in a bill of six short plays by James, Molnar, de Musset, Strindberg, Chekov, and Margaret Turner was a welcome relief from the parts she was usually given. The discriminating Maltese readily accepted her in such serious portrayals as the one she played in Henry James' *The American Wife.*

With Stringer she wandered hand-in-hand through the winding streets of Valletta, enjoying the potted plants with which each window ledge was loaded and the many friendly children who followed them, Pied Piper fashion, wherever they went. The management of the Manoel Theatre was delighted when Margaret complimented it upon having the cleanest backstage that she had ever seen.

When the season closed they stayed on for a few days of relaxation and swimming, joined by an old friend of mine, Roger Pain, a photographer from Heathfield, Sussex.

Back in England, Croydon playgoers and critics did not care for the collection of plays that had been so well received in Malta. The cast performed on an experimental round stage, where Margaret personally found the side view of Stringer, playing Chekov's lecturer on the harmfulness of tobacco, "rather magnificent."

Stringer clipped the following critical comment for their scrapbook: "Half the pleasure of watching Miss Margaret Rutherford is to see the play of life on that superb mug; the back of her wig is less impressive."

Mother wrote me, as if consoling herself: "If Croydon was not too keen on us, the audiences at Bath were more appreciative."

Nineteen hundred sixty-one proved to be a happy year, for it was then that she received her O.B.E. (Officer of the Order of the British Empire), from Queen Elizabeth II. It marked the first of several pleasant visits to Buckingham Palace. At one of the Queen's luncheons, Her Majesty said: "I am going to give you a great honor, Miss Rutherford. It is my husband's birthday and you are going to sit beside him."

Prince Philip responded with a smile. "And now, Miss Rutherford," he replied, "we can really talk about the theater."

They did, lighting on several other subjects as well. The Queen's husband wanted to know, "Why do you call Stringer 'Tuft'?"

Afterward Margaret was invited to have coffee with the Royal Family in their private sitting room. In came Princess Anne, home for midterm from Beneden School. She had a large pile of autograph books gathered from all her friends, including her own. Very politely she said: "Please, Miss Rutherford, will you kindly sign them?"

The somewhat embarrassed Queen interrupted: "Oh, darling, you can't do that to Miss Rutherford."

"Nonsense," said Mother, foraging in her large handbag. "Bother, I cannot find my fountain pen."

Prince Philip soon remedied the situation with one of his own.

In the midst of such exciting goings-on, Mother was worrying about me. Cousin Isabel had suffered a slight stroke, which had impaired her sense of color so that she was no longer able to paint with any certainty. Weak and listless on some days, she could not take her daily walk as she had always done, despite her crippled leg. At the same time, my biography of Isabel's collateral ancestress, Ann Hasseltine Judson, first American woman missionary to Burma, had become a major book club selection. Deciding that here was my chance to do something for Isabel, with the considerable advance I bought the Doctor Joseph Johnson House at Fifty-six Society Street in Charleston, South Carolina. There, at least during the winter months, Isabel could have enjoyed the walled garden in privacy, as a respite from New York City's cold.

Unfortunately she never lived to see the new acquisition. I found myself running a three-ring circus in the Tenth Street house, with the help of round-the-clock nurses. They were a motley collection. One set the drawing room chimney on fire and then rescued herself instead of the patient, while the last, and most helpful, looked like Gracie Allen and had her bookie bring the racing slips right up the steps to our Medusa Doorway. If it had not been for a fine woman physician, Dr. Parks McComb, who made house calls, and our mutual friend, Marion Foster, I would not have been able to have seen Isabel through her ordeal. She died quietly one afternoon while "Gracie Allen" was having her supper; by the time the nurse had finished eating, I had closed Isabel's eyes and put two quarters upon them.

Three days before her death, Isabel had decided that she did not wish her ashes to be placed under the granite obelisk in the family plot in Brooklyn's historic Greenwood Cemetery. Instead she had expressed a preference to rest beside my grandmother in England. As I had had no experience in dealing with American undertakers and our good friend, actress Joan Crawford, had, she was called in to help me. Joan had recently buried her nice husband, Alfred Steele, the Pepsi-Cola executive. She was a match for any funeral director as she was incapable of showing outward emotion except on the screen. She was also a Christian Scientist with a deep respect for Isabel's wishes. She handed the undertaker the nightgown that Isabel's mother had made for her trousseau in 1877 and dared him to say that she couldn't be buried in it.

The funeral tea was quite impressive, there being only one minor eruption. Said Mother: "Joan, dear, if you must serve

Pepsi-Cola, kindly refrain from using the Rockingham tea-cups."

The Reverend Thomas Savins, vicar of the Old Heathfield parish, conducted the funeral service. He had received minute instructions from Isabel's cousin, John Hay Whitney, as to how to fold the American flag with which the casket had been draped.

Of all the many floral tributes that Isabel received, only Mother's noted that she was being buried on St. Valentine's Day, the Festival of Love. Attached to Margaret's wreath was a large and rather gaudy red cardboard heart!

·8·
Mother

" IF they raised the taxes once again I was determined to march on the Houses of Parliament to protest and then if necessary, go to jail!"

Father was quite upset, for the last time she had threatened such a foray it had taken a personal call from Winston Churchill to stop her.

Mother had never been good with money: "hopeless" was her own description.

"The only reason that I want it is so that I can enjoy Elm Close with Tuft and our family . . . and of course help old friends."

The Internal Revenue people had their own ideas; they were out for blood. Many other celebrities had left Britain for tax-sheltered lives in Switzerland and the Caribbean but to my Mother, deserting Britain was out of the question.

Noel Coward told her that like him, she should find "a

143

warm little spot in Jamaica" and enjoy a well-earned old age in comfort. She was furious at the suggestion.

Instead, Mother forbade her accountant to pay the tax people another penny. He was to tell them bluntly: "Miss Rutherford will work as she did before. You will be paid in full."

The best offer that she received was the part of Miss Jane Marple, Agatha Christie's famed woman detective, in *Murder She Said,* a film that MGM planned to make in England.

For years, and with very good reason considering the tragedy of her father, something that her public did not know about, she had refused to take any role connected with crime. Sitting in the garden at Elm Close, sipping our tea from Rockingham cups, she was visibly disturbed at the prospect. "I hate violence of any kind and murder in particular," she declared so loudly that the sparrows that Father was feeding flew off in horror. "Besides, my public expects something better of me; they might not approve of a Rutherford Sherlock Holmes."

Time has proved her wrong, so much so that recently the regent of a New York chapter of the Daughters of the American Revolution introduced me as Miss Marple's daughter! Next to Madame Acarti, Miss Marple is Margaret's best remembered role.

For several days the three of us argued the pros and cons of poor Miss Marple. It was the principal topic of our 3 A.M. bacon-and-egg suppers. Just when Father and I thought that we had Mother's mind made up, she would suddenly come up with another excuse: "Perhaps we should phone Vicar Tom Savins. I would not want to be excommunicated."

Finally she was persuaded to read the David Pursall and Jack Seddon script adapted from Miss Christie's *4:50 from Paddington.* Mother was agreeably surprised, noting that Miss Marple "was obviously a good woman." There was a further incentive and perhaps the most important of all: Father had been offered the part of the village librarian, Miss Marple's trusted assistant. For once he would be given a role worthy of his talents. Writer Alison Uttley told Mother very convincingly that "the script does have a moral value of a sort."

Then the proposed film's director, George Pollock, diplomatically suggested that solving a murder was something like playing chess. These, together with none-too-gentle reminders from the Inland Revenue man, "that despicable ogre" as Father called him, finally worked the miracle.

On Christmas Day 1960, while Father was cooking the turkey, Mother phoned George Pollock. "This is Miss Rutherford speaking," she said in her loveliest voice. "I would be honored to play Miss Jane Marple." Pollock said that it was the best Christmas gift that he had received.

Although writer Ken Wlaschin said "she was brilliantly cast as Miss Marple," Agatha Christie was far from happy that Margaret Rutherford had been chosen for the role. She complained that the woman detective had been based upon her favorite aunt, a little woman who did not look a bit like Mother. Later, when actress and author finally met on the set, they liked each other immediately, becoming such good friends that Miss Christie dedicated her new mystery, *The Mirror Cracked from Side to Side,* to "my friend, Margaret Rutherford." Ironically, today the Christie heirs use Mother's picture to advertise new editions of Miss Marple mysteries.

Murder She Said begins with Miss Marple hurrying to catch a train. The scene was actually filmed on location at Paddington Station, where bona fide passengers stopped to watch Margaret Rutherford instead of concentrating on their own destinations. Several missed their trains.

Dressed as railway platelayers in outsized workmen's overalls and forage caps, Mother and Father enacted their favorite scene upon the local embankment at Gerrards Cross where the former said that she looked like "the Michelin tyre man's big sister." Father was more specific. "At last we have done something for the village," said he.

Although Wlaschin says that "the films themselves could have been better," the series of four Miss Marple movies proved immensely popular, pushing a somewhat bewildered Mother to the top of MGM's payroll.

Melvin Maddock's *Christian Science Monitor* review pleased both my parents. He wrote:

> One had an impression of frumpy hair fringed above baleful eyes and a permanently reproachful mouth. A formidably blocky torso stands draped in a regular tarpaulin of a sweater, descending over a tweedy skirt of indefinite length beneath which protrude two dangerously thin legs based hopefully upon sensible walking shoes. The effect is of a warmly bundled English bulldog.

There was a wonderful cover picture in the *New York Herald Tribune*'s Sunday entertainments magazine. It showed Mother and Father gingerly looking over the top of the embankment. Dominated by Miss Marple's ample figure, one could see very little of her assistant sleuth. Somewhat apologetically the caption read: "The eye belongs to Stringer Davis."

Taxes paid, they were now able to enjoy Elm Close, adding what they called The Children's Room at the top of the house. Mother persuaded an artist, whose name she could never remember, to paint special murals on the walls that were more suitable to the Roaring Twenties than to our own generation. Father bought three birdhouses for the garden and a new typewriter for himself. Fan mail was arriving by the sackful, much of it simply addressed to "Miss Marple." Poor Father answered it between cooking the bacon and eggs.

Elm Close was not an old house as houses go, but it was a

gracious home with good clean lines. The trees in front gave it the appearance of being in a wood. "We chose it because of the fairy snowdrop ring in the garden," said Mother.

There was indeed a fairy snowdrop ring, which always saw fit to bloom when snow was actually on the ground. At such time we all bundled up in heavy coats where, from under several layers of woollen shawls and eiderdowns, we were expected to take morning coffee at a little table set up beside it. Mother never felt the cold and could not understand why her guests, particularly the Americans used to their warm, centrally heated homes, did not appreciate "the beautiful fresh air."

Inside was more cozy, for there was a large inglenook fireplace where she liked to sit and read poetry aloud, pausing every so often to poke the coals burning in the open grate.

Everywhere was an eclectic array of personal treasures. These had been collected on their farflung travels and were happily mixed with priceless antiques inherited from Stringer's mother, who cast a somewhat disapproving eye from her portrait in an oval gilt frame that was always falling to pieces at the wrong time. Once when the senior Mrs. Davis fell out of her frame in the middle of Mother's reading Cathy's death scene from Wuthering Heights, she looked at me and said, "Sometimes I think that Tuft's mother does it on purpose!"

The garden was Father's personal domain, and in particular one tall and rather straggly pink rose bush, from which, even in the dead of winter, he always seemed able to coax a bloom.

Their good friend Robert Morley provides a word picture of my parents at this satisfying domestic period in their lives:

> On country walks together he was reported to pluck bouquets from the hedge rows and present them to her on his knees which must have got rather muddy, but I like better

the story of when he was cooking bacon and eggs for her in the kitchen and no one must interrupt him with loud conversations in the adjoining room!

Robert should have been there while Stringer was cooking John-Paul's and my wedding breakfast. We were obliged to speak in whispers!

Although it was widely reported in the media that at this period in their lives Father always served Mother breakfast wearing a spacesuit, I never saw him do it. What I can vouch for is that he wore striped white pajamas and a camel's hair dressing gown, while Mother was prone to shocking-pink robes and sensible flannelette nightgowns. Once they both wanted to cook breakfast for me and, rather than fall out on such a domestic note, each prepared a tray. With smiling faces, Mother still in her beribboned snooze-net, they appeared in my bedroom, each carrying a well-laden tray that included three large daisies, each in a silver vase. I soon discovered that it was not easy to balance a breakfast tray on each knee!

Their friends were as varied as their possessions. While Mother held court like a queen in the garden, "Tuft," as she wrote, "nobly created our lunch." Of such an occasion, Dora Seimons, a cherished friend to whom Mother always sent tickets for her plays, recalls: "Once in the garden at Elm Close, upon Stringer calling us into lunch, Margaret said to me, 'Dora, darling, I like talking to you!' A great compliment. There has never been an artiste of her calibre. She was so natural. Her art was of the kind that concealed art. She once said to me: 'I never play for laughs'."

At Gerrards Cross the neighbors respected her privacy. The butcher called her "Mrs. Davis," which she loved, and she was on a first-name basis with the vicar, whom she liked to have over for afternoon tea. After one such a visit, she puckered her lips with mock relish, and exclaimed: "He really enjoys my cream buns."

It was on a perfect summer day that I set out with my parents to visit the graves of William Penn and his two wives, Gulielma and Hannah, in the Quaker burial ground at Jordans Meeting House. The long walk from Elm Close had a dual purpose. I was gathering information for a magazine article on the first Mrs. Penn. Guli, as she was known in her family, was the daughter of Sir William Springett of Broyle Place, Ringmer—in my generation the home of Anthony Dawson, actor and one of my daughter Natasha's godfathers. Guli was celebrated for her beauty, wit, and many accomplishments; although she did not live to visit America, her daughter, Letitia, did.

Standing by her grave with the sweet smell of new mown hay in the air was a rare experience for the Davis family. We just stood quietly, holding hands.

That night in the inglenook, Mother decided that William Penn must have been thinking of his beloved Guli, the bride of his youth, when he wrote: "They that love beyond the world cannot be separated. Death cannot kill what never dies. Death is but crossing the world as friends do the seas: they live in one another still."

One of the pleasures of making the Miss Marple pictures so close to home was that Margaret and Stringer could often drive to the studio in the early morning by pony and trap.

Because of the popularity of these Agatha Christie movies in America, Mother was often interviewed by reporters from New York. One young man arrived at Elm Close at tea-time and was promptly invited to join the family. He was fascinated with the big china teapot and the lack of teabags.

"These tea breaks are so much a part of our daily lives that I'd feel quite unable to go on without them," Mother confessed.

Then the reporter commented on the teacups, which were gigantic, even by British standards, edged with bands of ma-

genta red and and dobs of white that looked just like Devonshire cream. "This is our strawberry service," she told him.
"My husband only allows me to use the Rockingham cups on
special family occasions."

Asked for her own reaction to Miss Marple, she said:

> At first I refused to take the role. Murder, you see, is not
> the sort of thing I could get close to. I don't like anything
> that tends to lower or debase or degrade. But then a friend
> and I talked it over, and she pointed out that it *could* be
> entertaining and might indeed have a moral value, of a sort
> . . . and one likes to throw one's weight in on the side of
> good, doesn't one?

The American reporter, his mouth full of buttered scone
and homemade raspberry jam, spluttered his complete
agreement.

Sunday luncheon was always a time of suspense at Elm
Close for we never knew quite what to expect. Right in the
middle of our treacle pudding or gooseberry pie, Mother
would gaily announce that we were all driving down to Maid-
stone Jail or some other criminal institution where she was to
give a reading to "the boys" . . . and or sometimes to "the
girls."

I did not know then why she was so fond of giving her
professional services to the prisoners on what could have
been her day of rest. She could command high fees for such
performances in some public hall. Reading her letters some
time after her death, I realized that what she was doing was in
memory of her father. "I like to think that somebody like
Mr. Gilpin the Quaker found time to read to him."

Standing on an impromptu stage with her splendidly large
and gaudy handbag propped up by a table leg, she would
literally bring down the walls of the jail when she recited
T. S. Eliot's "Macavity's a mystery cat . . ." She led her
captive audience into her own wonderful world of fantasy as

she rapidly changed herself into a variety of extraordinary beings.

"Then I turned myself into porridge," she says, "blub, blub, heaving and spluttering and plonking. I have been out-methoding the Method School of Acting since I was a child. That is what acting is all about."

When John Carroll arranged a poetry reading at Penton-ville Prison, Mother was his star attraction. "It was a full house," she said, with obvious relish, "about nine hundred and fifty of them, for the Governor had popped in all the worst offenders as well. It was a very tough, grim audience who were all wondering what they were going to hear . . . You could have heard a pin drop during my recital of 'The Lady of Shalott'."

It was like old times when she returned to Holloway, next door to where she had lived in her bedsitter after Aunt Bessie died. She was to read and recite in the women's prison there and this time had no Rumer Godden to guide her in the choice of a suitable program. Just before entering the hall where she was to perform, the prison governor casually asked her what she intended to recite first. "Oh, 'The Shooting of Dan McGrew'," she said!

"It was a good blood-curdling bit which I thought the poor women would enjoy as they must have been a little disillusioned by the men in their lives" was her later explanation.

With a great deal of tact, the governor managed to convince her that "Dan McGrew" was not quite suitable in those surroundings.

It was during 1962 when Mother was appearing in *The School for Scandal* at the Royal Haymarket that she felt herself privileged to meet the ghost of John B. Buckstone.

Afraid of missing a matinee the next day because of a train slowdown (my parents traveled to London by train from Gerrards Cross), she asked the theater management if they might spend the night in her dressing room. When the building's fireman grumbled that it would be against the rules, Mother stood firm and announced, "Rules are meant to be broken."

With Stringer sleeping on the folding camp bed that they had brought into the city with the anticipation of staying over, and Mother curled up on the comfortable sofa, they were perfectly happy. In the middle of the night Mother awoke. "I had a vision," she said. "Coming out of the closet, which would not close because of my voluminous dresses, was a very hairy leg. This was followed by a face I immediately recognized as belonging to John Buckstone, the eighteenth-century actor-manager. I wasn't a bit frightened, and neither do I think was he. Mr. Buckstone had obviously been admiring my dresses, which of course belonged to his period of time. He must have felt quite at home."

Father slept right through the ghost's visit. In the morning he was quite vexed to have missed it.

In 1978, Anthony Peek wrote me from the same theater that "we do not have a ghost of Garrick at this theatre, but J. B. Buckstone, a former manager and great favorite of Her Majesty Queen Victoria, has been seen."

Mother enjoyed making *Murder at the Gallop,* her second Miss Marple film, as her co-star was her cherished friend Robert Morley. The scene at the end where she refuses his proposal of matrimony and his subsequent exclamation, "What an escape!" when he realizes that she is against all blood sports and in particular fox hunting, was a masterpiece of facial expressions from both of them.

To LIFE she later confessed: "I didn't really ride that horse in *Murder at the Gallop.* The only time I ever rode was when I was two or three in India. I had a white pony."

If she had not played Grand Duchess Gloriana XIII in the

space-race spoof, *Mouse on the Moon,* Mother and Father would not have found themselves at Cape Canaveral, Florida, in 1962, visiting the American astronauts.

The film's plot was centered around Duchy of Grand Fenwick's chief physicist, delightfully played by David Kossoff, who by chance discovers that the little country's famed wine, which keeps exploding, is the perfect rocket fuel. Suddenly the sleepy duchy is propelled into the space age.

Mother enjoyed the experience of acting with Kossoff so much that to the end of her days she treasured a fan letter that he wrote her. It was found in Aunt Bessie's old steamer trunk and went like this:

> I have been an admirer of yours almost as long as I can remember. I have seen you in many things. You are a unique performer. This half lunatic technique which you have made your own is the product of art. You always know precisely what you are doing.
>
> You even know what to do with your body and your head in the most astonishing way. When other people make faces you use that heavy chin and that wide-set eye look. I have always admired the way you know what to do with your body. You have looked at this with remarkable honesty but there is not a muscle that escapes your notice. I like the economy of your movements, how you never waste energy. I have always thought that the sign of quality in a performer is economy, and this you have in very full measure.

Astronaut Scott Carpenter also wrote her a fan letter, saying how much he would like her autograph for each of his four children.

Mouse on the Moon had its American premiere at Cape Canaveral, where after the performance Mother was formally introduced to fellow astronauts L. Gordon Cooper, Jr., and Walter M. Schirra, Jr. She was particularly gratified during the movie by the hearty laughter of an audience made up of astronauts, officers, technicians, and their wives and families.

Later, in the intimacy of the hotel swimming pool, my parents became friendly with the astronauts themselves. When Mother said how much more she enjoyed swimming in the real ocean, Cooper and his two daughters gladly accompanied them, together with Buttons, the Coopers' swimming cat. Buttons, his master told them, had been a water enthusiast since kitten days.

Back in New York City for a private showing of the movie, Mother and Father were wined and dined regally by United Artists. Because of the time differences they were experiencing, Mother craved her cup of tea at the oddest hours. Unfortunately they had left Elm Close in such a hurry that Father had forgotten to pack their precious teapot. Even at the Plaza, tea was not served in the middle of the night, but officials at United Artists, who had produced *Mouse on the Moon*, "gallantly came to our rescue," Mother said. A member of the Plaza's staff volunteered to come in early at 6:30 in the morning so that the Grand Duchess Gloriana could have her cup of tea.

While in New York, Mother appeared on Johnny Carson's *Tonight* show. He reminded her of "a young man I used to know in repertory at Croydon."

Hermione Baddeley took her for tea at the Russian Tea Room, a "most sensible and thoughtful choice," Father duly noted, while United Artists gave them both a farewell party at Sardi's. "Can you believe it," gushed Mother, "that very lovable man, Vincent Sardi, has been our friend since *The Importance of Being Earnest.*"

As I was sick at the time, I missed all of the fun both in Cape Canaveral and New York.

Mother wrote:

Dearest Child:
   It was most frustrating flying over what surely must have

been your home in Charleston. If I could, I would have parachuted down to see you.

The British press reported during her Marple period that she was the highest-paid actress in the country.

In 1963 she again had "that dear man," Robert Morley, as her co-star in another of the Miss Marple series, *Murder Most Foul.* Later, in *Murder Ahoy,* Mother had to fight a duel with swords, and for a woman who did not like violence in any form, acquitted herself quite well. For some reason she never had the opportunity of seeing this film on the screen, a personal disappointment.

Because of Miss Marple's popularity in America, director Anthony Asquith asked Mother to play the doughty Duchess of Brighton in *The V.I.P.'s,* a film he was to make with Elizabeth Taylor and her then husband, Richard Burton. Although Mother admired Asquith's talent as a director, calling him "that man of gentle manners and sheer brilliance," after reading the script and discovering that her role had "no background or meat for me to get my teeth into," she politely refused it. To his credit, Asquith respected her judgment and called in the producer, Anatole de Grunwald, and the scriptwriter, Terence Rattigan. The result was a new Duchess of Brighton, with, as Mother said, "both substance and integrity."

The Duchess of Brighton was a penniless noblewoman who had been forced to take a social director's job with a Miami Beach hotel because she could no longer pay her taxes. For Mother this was all very ironic and she played her scenes to the hilt, getting the best laugh when she addressed the airplane flight attendant as "conductress," just as if she were riding on a double-decker bus!

Mother enjoyed acting with Elizabeth Taylor whose fan she had been for a long time. With Father she had sat through the movie of Caesar and Cleopatra three times! She thought that Elizabeth "was a much misunderstood girl whose only fault was that she loved too deeply." The competition between the Burtons was apparent to everyone on the set. Mother described it perfectly:

> It's no secret that they both can act beautifully but at times it became a "who-is-the-better?" contest. Elizabeth would play a scene to the very hilt and make it the zenith of perfection. Richard would then come along and try to top it with his own brand of dynamism. They would then ask me to select the winner. This was rather hard, having to choose between my favorite Caesar and Cleopatra!

When Mother won an Academy Award for the Best Supporting Actress of 1963 for her role as the Duchess of Brighton, the Burtons sent her a cable of congratulations.

In time Oscar had pride of place on the inglenook mantelpiece at Elm Close. Next to it she placed a photograph of all three of us in a little golden frame. It had been taken by Margaret Savins, wife of the then Vicar of Old Heathfield.

As Mother and Father were both staunch admirers of President and Mrs. John F. Kennedy, Mother was delighted to write me on August 9, 1963: "We are exhilarated at knowing that Jacqueline Kennedy has placed a copy of your new book in the library at the White House." This was my biography, *Vinnie Ream—the Girl Who Sculptured Lincoln.* She was equally impressed when Mrs. Kennedy sent an aide down to my home in Charleston to see if I would give my pair of George Washington mirrors to the executive mansion.

Mother liked to boast that she had once received a love letter from Marlon Brando. At least *she* called it a love letter!

Marlon was very kind, allowing her the use of his large, comfortable dressing room, right on the edge of the set. It was there on the first day of filming her scenes in *The Countess of Hong Kong* that she found Marlon's delightfully boyish letter awaiting her. "Oh," she exclaimed, clapping her hands with all the excitment of a young girl, "I must tell Vivien

Leigh. I know it sounds rather naughty but I did enjoy the scene where Marlon seduced her in *A Streetcar Named Desire.*"

Father, who once while decorating our Christmas tree, confessed that he would far rather have been a clown than an actor, had always been a fan of Charlie Chaplin. He was very excited when Chaplin invited Mother and him for cocktails at the Savoy.

Chaplin had personally chosen Mother for her cameo role of the old lady who stays in bed, surrounded by stuffed animals, all through a luxury cruise in his production of *The Countess of Hong Kong.*

Both my parents were impressed by the warmth of the welcome given them by Chaplin and his wife, Oona. Said Mother: "Her gentleness pervaded the room like potpourri." Chaplin went out of his way to convince Mother that her part, though small, was an important one. "Besides," he said, "my own part is even smaller. I am to play a ship's steward."

Father had brought along a copy of Chaplin's autobiography, which Mother had given him. Chaplin read aloud her inscription: "To my favorite Clown, Guide, and Counselor, Friend and Husband with the everlasting love of Eternal Things, Margaret."

Chaplin picked up a pen and wrote underneath: "May I endorse Margaret's statement, Chaplin."

Although *The Countess of Hong Kong* won little critical acclaim, it was one film that Mother never regretted making. Her own cameo performance did not go unnoticed. Nicholas Kostis, a lecturer on films at Boston University, wrote: "It was worth sitting through the sheer boredom of *The Countess of Hong Kong* for two hours just to see Margaret Rutherford."

On a gray, wintry morning early in 1964, my parents drove down to Beecholme, Old Heathfield, former home of my grandmother, Nelly Hall Ticehurst, and of her Spanish mother, Martha (Marta) Hall. Martha had had it built several hundred feet above sea level in the 1890s; it had stunning views of the South Downs and the English Channel. The house then belonged to me.

Mother Rutherford, who liked to plant trees "for the benefit of future generations," had decided to plant a poplar, one of the tallest of trees, as her contribution to the property. She arrived wearing a sensible black-and-white-checked woolen coat with a green headscarf. With Father in the rear smoking his usual cigarette, I walked her up the garden path past the graves of Isabel's pet turtle, Lizzie, and Clementine, the Amazon parrot who had preceded Marilyn. Their ashes had been sent over for burial from New York.

"Ah," said mother, pausing as if searching for the right words, "they are in their little spirit boxes."

After walking through a wrought-iron gate and into the windy field where we kept the three black and white mountain sheep Ronald, Ethel, and Eleanor, given me by Vita Sackville-West, we found a small crowd of villagers awaiting us. Mary Jane Kemp, eighty-six and well bundled up in an enormous woolen scarf, had a posy of pink Portsmouth cabbage and violets for Mother, while another bunch of early spring flowers was given her by Philip Savins, younger son of the Vicar of Old Heathfield. Both Mrs. Kemp and Philip were heartily kissed by Mother. Then, with Father holding on to his trilby hat, for the wind from the channel was strong, Mother went to work with a vengeance, while I held the poplar in place.

Most people, when planting a ceremonial tree, just spade a handful of dirt around it, leaving the gardener to finish the job. Not my mother!

"When you plant a tree," she shouted, while her audience shivered, "you plant it properly." The tree lived and one day will be a landmark for miles!

Afterward we were joined by the Reverend Thomas Savins, who had recited a few prayers at the planting, and his cheerful wife, Margaret, whom I've never heard say an unkind word about anyone in all the years I have known her. We all had lunch in an old country inn at East Hoathly, a few miles away. Every winter since, when the trees are bare of their leaves, I always think of Mother, and her words as we drove past Broyle Place, Guli Penn's old home: "I love the trees best of all in winter. Their branches seem to reach right up into heaven like the tracery in a cathedral ceiling."

We were accompanied at lunch by Roger Pain, the photographer who had enjoyed daily swims with my parents in Malta, and whose record of the occasion now rests with our papers in the William R. Perkins Library at Duke University. Mother had always wanted to work the handles that controlled the flow of beer behind the bar, so there was no peace until she tried her hand at being a barmaid with Tom Savins, the vicar, making a good bartender beside her. "Just like working the chance machines on Eastbourne Pier," she exclaimed estatically.

The afternoon ended with a visit to Cauldomer, Marle Green, the red brick home of my cousins Alfred and Rosamanda Stanton. When I was young, Rosy, as she was known in the family, always had time for the lonely child I then was. She called us "the outcasts" and lifted me up onto her fire truck to go for a ride. By profession she was a fire fighter and a very good one too, so it seemed appropriate that she should present Mother with a model of a fire truck as a memento of the occasion.

"We will place it on our bedroom mantelpiece," said Father, like a small boy with a new toy.

Tea was served close by at Vine's Cross Bakery, where Mother told Burton Harriot, the baker: "I like bread to have really hard crusts. Soft mushy bread is no good for our stomachs or our teeth. Both need exercise!"

Mother and Father were later to pay another happy visit to Old Heathfield, this time in mid-summer when mother unveiled the stained glass window I had commissioned in memory of my grandmother and her twin sister, Aunty Doom. It is known as an Anglo-American Friendship Window for it commemorates a former vicar of All Saints, Old Heathfield, who in 1607 became chaplain to the original Jamestown settlement in Virginia. It was designed by Laurence Lee, the artist-designer responsible for the splendid glass in Coventry Cathedral when it was rebuilt after the bombing in World War II.

In the Anglo-American Friendship window, Lee had portrayed Grandmother and Aunty's childhood faces superimposed upon those of two Indian children, representative of Virginia's original inhabitants. They were taken from an old Victorian photograph made on Brighton Beach.

Tom Savins, who was complimented by Mother for his "most beautiful reading voice . . . rather like Larry Olivier's," invited her up into the pulpit where she read verses from Hebrews, Chapter 11, her own choice:

> From henceforth expecting 'til His enemies be made His footstool.
> For by one offering He hath perfected for ever them that are sanctified

Mother particularly liked Tom Savins' sermon, in which he aptly noted "All up and down the country are windows commemorating lords and ladies, admirals and generals, but ours is different. It has been given in memory of two housewives."

"Tony could not have expressed it better," said Mother later.

As for religion, she told Tom: "I have deep spiritual feelings and so does my husband."

Afterward there were two teas, one at Beecholme and another at the Vicarage. Both Mother and Cousin Madge Butler, a farmer and co-matron of a nursing home, were partial to little iced cakes. "This is my last. Three teacakes are just too much, even for my figure," said Mother.

"Too much?" shouted Cousin Madge who was just as large. "I have just eaten my seventh."

Mother in her own way had now become a much-loved public figure, as illustrated by the story that her old neighbor and friend Rumer Godden tells so well:

My husband retired and we left Old Hall but thank God, we were not to lose Margaret and Stringer. She went to America where she came into her own. Margaret and Stringer came down to Dusgrove in Sussex, the old house that we had renovated, for the weekend. She had to be back in London for rehearsal at 10 o'clock on the Monday morning. She loved the peace, the gardens and the woods so much that she decided to stay and catch the 8 o'clock from Hastings on Monday.

We stayed up late the night before, James and Stringer recalling the old Music Hall days, playing and singing. There was one tune whose title and lyrics Stringer couldn't remember. I warned James that Margaret and Stringer had to be up at six in order to catch the train, that they had quite a little drive to the station.

Promptly at 6 o'clock, I woke them with their morning tea and then left them to dress. When at seven there was still no sign of either of them, I went back upstairs to investigate. Stringer was dressed but Margaret stood in her dressing gown, their belongings strewn all over the room. By some miracle I managed to get them packed, Margaret dressed and downstairs.

"I must not be late," said Margaret. I think in all her professional life she was very seldom late. Just as they were getting into the car, Stringer suddenly said, "I remember," got out of the car, rushed into the drawing room to the piano and began singing the words of "365 Days"!

We arrived at Hastings just as the train was due to leave. James had a word with the ticket collector, then there were long steps to climb. Eventually we arrived on the platform with Margaret, her cloak streaming in the wind, having the station master in attendance. The porter followed with all their bags and we found a carriage. We were assured that they would get breakfast on the train, yet instead of getting in in a hurry, Margaret turned and with quiet dignity first said goodbye and thank you to me and then to James. She then thanked the porter and shook hands with the station master, then gracefully made her exit into the carriage.

Were doors slammed open and shut? No, they stayed open! Were whistles blown? Did people get impatient? Not a bit of it. Everyone watched entranced and I think there might have been a clap of applause as eventually the train drew out. It was just typical of the great love that everyone who saw her felt and got in return from Margaret.

"Television," Mother said, "is a medium I find both fascinating and exhausting."

In 1964 she was the blessed choice of NBC to appear in their television special *The Stately Ghosts of England.* Three of Britain's great houses, Longleat, Beaulieu, and Salisbury, were chosen as authentic locations. Mother, as hostess with her green capes, flowing gowns, and beautiful hats, filled the role to perfection.

Tom Corbett, the leading British clairvoyant, had written the book from which a script was adapted. When the producer wanted Mother to be "funny," she absolutely refused, knowing that to take Corbett's work lightly might easily ruin his reputation.

Of actual ghosts she said: "I am prepared to acknowledge that there is something outside my knowledge and understanding."

During the filming the ghosts seem to have kept their distance, except at Longleat where the cameras recorded a small ball of light flying down a long corridor. Corbett tactfully explained that such light appears before a spirit materialization. Later, when the cutting room editors deleted it, Mother was furious, while Father grumbled: "Most authentic part of the whole thing."

Both parents enjoyed visiting the stately homes and meeting their owners. Mother was photographed pretending to drive an antique car in the Motor Museum at Beaulieu; the photo was later produced on a picture postcard. In real life she never learned to drive, and neither did Father.

Mother harbored a secret ambition to appear in the play *The Solid Gold Cadillac* by Howard Teichmann and George S. Kaufman. Maybe it was her own troubles with the income tax people that made the part of Mrs. Laura Partridge so appealing.

"I would play her as an artful battleaxe," she told me one afternoon over tea in the garden at Elm Close. She wanted to know what I thought of the idea. Josephine Hull, an actress much admired by Mother, had created the role in the original Broadway production, while the much younger Judy Holliday had played it on the screen.

I told her quite truthfully that I thought the story was just too American for a British audience, but she was quite adamant.

"She just wants to wear that beautiful pair of gold overalls" was Father's comment.

Arthur Lee, who had made his name with *Little Me,* was the director, and in due course *The Solid Gold Cadillac* opened for tryouts in Birmingham complete with a revolving stage.

"Arthur assured me that if I stayed still I would end up in the right place," said Mother. In desperation she wrote me that the dress rehearsal was "chaotic . . . only your Father Stringer could give me the moral courage I needed. Thank God he has the role of secretary to the big company."

Father added a P.S.: "That solid gold suit is simply unbelievable. Your Mother looks like the Bank of England."

Each night she went straight from the theater to a local nursing home, "to," as she wrote, "recharge my batteries."

A few weeks later her nerves gave out, sending her into fits of crying and agitation. She managed to pull herself together for the London opening but it was just too much, and *The Solid Gold Cadillac* collapsed with her.

Mary Margaret Fuller, Managing Editor of FATE magazine, was in England at the time with Tom Corbett as tour guide. She was to have seen Mother in the play only to be told that her health had suddenly broken down. She was very disappointed and so were many other regular Rutherford fans. *The Solid Gold Cadillac* was something that she had really wanted to do. It was important to her morale; she never quite forgave herself for the play's premature demise.

She was again taken to a nursing home in a terrible state, so that we feared for her sanity. Poor Father had to face newspapers for she had long ago become like Big Ben, a British institution. Bravely he told the London *Daily Mirror* on June 5, 1965: "She is suffering from an agitated depression. She is under deep sedation."

As on previous occasions, Mother gradually came out of her lethargy and Father took her home to the place they both loved best, Elm Close. She was then seventy-three years old.

In 1966 she still felt "tired and overwrought" and begged me to come home and make her, of all people, "laugh." I was in the middle of my research for a most taxing biography, *William, Father of the Netherlands,* but I promised that I would come as soon as I could.

Fortunately Sir John Clements, whom she had known years before, repeated Robert Morley's role as "doctor."

"He raised me from my lethargy as he had done once before in 1956," Mother later said. On that occasion, when she was suffering from another of her mental breakdowns, Sir John had firmly told her that work was the "best and only therapy" and, in her no-nonsense British way, she believed him. In no time at all he had had her rehearsing *The Way of the World,* which, she confessed, "revitalized" her.

Now he wanted her to perform on the new round stage at Chichester in Sussex, in Colman and Garrick's period piece, *The Clandestine Marriage.* "You will have the most beautiful costumes," he promised, knowing that with her weakness for dressing up she could not resist him.

In his letter written in longhand from the Lyric Theatre, December 28, 1965, Sir John says:

> Dearest Margaret,
>
> As I expect you know, Larry [Laurence Olivier] gives up the direction of the theatre at Chichester at the end of this week when I officially take over from him. And I am, of course, already in the throes of planning my first season. An exciting but alarming project! To follow Larry and the National Theatre Company is a challenge of rather enormous proportions!
>
> I cannot tell you what delight it would give me if I could persuade you to come and play in my first season. In fact what I would dearly love is that you should play in the opening play! It has just got to be something that starts the new regime on the right note, and the more I think of it the more sure I am that it should be an evening of gaiety and, above all, of style.
>
> There is no-one to whom those two words apply more than they do to you!
>
> The question is, of course, what play? My first thought was "The Rivals," but I did it in my season at the Saville and I feel it would be a mistake for that reason, much as I would love to do it again, especially with you.
>
> And then I re-read "The Clandestine Marriage." I had forgotten what a delicious play it is! If you will play Mrs. Heidelberg I shall settle, with happiness and excitement, for that!"

There were to be seven weeks of rehersals, so, with Father and all their paraphanalia, including his typewriter (for he was about two years behind in answering her fan mail), they moved to the pleasant confines of the Beach Hotel in Little-hampton. There they enjoyed long walks by the sea, informal teas with photographer Roger Pain, and, of course, swim-ming. It was an easy drive to Chichester for rehearsals.

Father even managed to catch up with some of the fan mail, which Mother dutifully signed in her exotic flowery handwriting. Boston film reviewer Albert Manski was some-what surprised to receive a reply to a letter he had written Mother two years previously. She blamed the delay on "pres-sure of work" and then proceeded to thank him for his "en-couragement."

After *The Claudestine Marriage* came the chance to act under the direction of Orson Welles, which could not be ignored. Also Mother had always wanted to go to Spain, particularly since I had come into her life. She had been intrigued with the biographical novel *The Gypsy Condesa* I had published on the life of the Condesa Elisabeta de Men-doza Harris, my great-great grandmother who at forty-two had married a boy of eighteen. She knew that the Condesa had been born in Triana, the gypsy section of Seville, and had then moved to Madrid where some of the filming of *Chimes at Midnight* would take place. She always said that she had much in common with the Condesa, who like herself could be described as a one-woman armada. "Oh, how I wish I could play your Condesa," she told me, "but I fear I am now too old." It was the only concession I ever heard her make to age.

She was to be paid the sum of eight thousand pounds for her part in the classic movie, with a generous daily living allowance as well. Alas! there was a slip-up, and although Father was written into the contract as being her "companion on the trip," at the last minute somebody forgot all about him. It took a delightfully soothing letter from Alessandro Tasca, the executive producer, to put matters right. "You will be pleased to hear that a solution has been found. . . . It had been overlooked that Miss Rutherford would be accompanied by her husand."

Based on the story of Falstaff from William Shakespeare, *Chimes at Midnight* proved a highlight in Mother's career. Orson Welles treated her royally; it was even written into her contract that her name should appear above the movie title in any advertising. It was a far cry from the days when she received ten guineas a week and three percent of the gross weekly box office receipts for her role as Mrs. Danvers in the play *Rebecca*. The publication *Classic Movie Stars* calls her role as Mistress Quickly in the Orson Welles film "possibly her very best."

Internacional Films, which made *Chimes at Midnight,* had the co-operation of Spanish military horses for the epic battle scenes. The precision of these horses reminded my parents of the studio horses they had seen in Hollywood and of Romulus and Remus, the white drays used in *Murder at the Gallop.* Said Mother: "The Spanish horses on the big open ground during the battle scene were trained in film work, in exactly the same way. I noticed that when the call for 'action' came, they went right into it in just the same way."

As for Orson Welles, she described him simply as "a gentleman."

Looking back, it is amazing the stamina that a woman of her age could muster after having suffered a nervous breakdown. Not satisfied with the excitement and satisfaction of filming in Spain, and with the fear always lurking at the back of her mind that her old adversary, the tax man, had his eye on her beloved Elm Close, she agreed to appear in the demanding part of Mrs. Malaprop in Richard Sheridan's play *The Rivals.* Sir Ralph Richardson, whom she called "the most irresistible man in the world with the exception of Stringer," persuaded her to take the role and so help launch the Haymarket Theatre Royal Company. She loved the gorgeous period costumes, the enormous powdered wigs, and the hats, including a folding bonnet called a *calash,* but best of all she loved the opening scene where she was carried onstage in a sedan chair.

I flew over to see her as Mrs. Malaprop, surprising her in her dressing room, where I would never have known her in the heavy makeup she was applying. Afterwards, as Mrs. Jones, the lady chauffeur, drove us all home to Elm Close at Gerrards Cross, she saw fit to complain: "Such a comedown from a golden sedan chair."

Although Mrs. Malaprop's classic misuse of the English language highlights the period play, Margaret readily admitted: "My memory was not as good as it had been." She celebrated her seventy-fifth birthday with an enormous iced cake on stage.

The critics were kind to her: "Her timing is judged to a hair as phrase after phrase wings like a new flight of doves from a billowy dovecot that is Mrs. Malaprop," wrote one.

In a letter dated April 22, 1967, she wrote me in Charleston: "I am much better now [she had had the flu] and the play is running happily on, in fact, on April 24th we shall have run longer than any other production of *The Rivals* since it was written!"

It was also a very sentimental play for me; I never had the courage to tell her that the only time I ever appeared onstage in my life was also in a production of *The Rivals,* given by the Winnipeg Little Theatre. I had a very small role and in the last scene had to sit on the shoulder of John Hirsch.

Mother always loved going to Buckingham Palace for as she said, "I have always been an admirer of our Royal Family and deplore the disrespect which some of the younger generation, and regrettably some newspapers, indulge in. I will have no part of it."

One of her favorite visits had been back in 1964 when the Queen had given a special reception for those connected with the theater to celebrate the four-hundredth anniversary of Shakespeare's birth.

Mother and Father attended with John Carroll who lived with them and had been invited because of his sensitive work with poetry at Stratford-on-Avon. They arrived early, and Mother, excited as a child, exclaimed: "Come along, Johnnie, we want to see everything." They carefully examined all of the State rooms that were open for the guests to see; as Mother said, "I didn't want to miss a thing."

Suddenly a door opened behind them and there was Queen Elizabeth and her retinue. Seeing Mother, the Queen walked over to greet her, while Mother in turn introduced her to Father and Johnnie. Father told Her Majesty that once, when Mother had returned from an informal luncheon with the Queen at Buckingham Palace, she had remarked to him "how pretty the Queen was."

Queen Elizabeth seemed genuinely touched. "Thank you," she said, while Mother noted that she was blushing.

"Of course all the Dames were there—Edith [Sitwell], Sybil [Thorndike], Flora [Robson], and dear Phyllis Nielson Terry. Most of the Knights were present, but Larry Olivier was rehearsing for *Othello* and could not make it. Ralph Richardson told me that he had forgotten his glasses so the name tags the guests were given to wear for easy identification were not much use to him."

Dame Flora Robson was particularly fond of Mother and in a letter to me dated October 28, 1980, had this to say about her:

> I think I only once acted with Margaret in a thriller film. I was the one who did the murder, I think she did the detective work. They found the film too long, and my best scene was cut. I think I was trying to vindicate myself in it. I did not make any fuss as I knew people watched the film

to see Margaret, but it was *she* who complained, saying my best scene was out!

I had a tremendous admiration for her. She was sincere and serious, NOT trying to be a comic. As she was rather eccentric she got all the laughs. But I learned from her to play my comedy seriously.

Another British star who was equally appreciative of Mother as an actress and a person was James Mason. Writing me November 11, 1981, from his home in Corseaux, Switzerland, he said: "It is true that I still have the habit of naming her as 'the best actress' that I ever worked with. I liked her and I admired her work enormously. In her later days there were many films in which her appearance was the only item which made them worth watching."

According to Mother, the two greatest days of her life were her wedding and January 1, 1967, when her name appeared in the New Year's Honors List. She was awarded her damehood. "Such an uplift" was her immediate reaction.

In due course she set off for Buckingham Palace with Stringer and John Carroll, who was now living on the top floor at Elm Close, something that pleased her very much. Jessie Pearce, who was then her dresser, came along "to see that there was not a speck of dust upon me and that everything was perfect."

Of that occasion, Mother recalled that the Queen wanted to know if she were making any new films. "I had the feeling that her sister, Princess Margaret, might have prompted her to ask me, for I had been told on several occasions that the Princess is very fond of my films."

Of the Queen, Mother said: "As I stood there and noted her perfect complexion, delphinium blue eyes, and warm smile, I thought, here is one human being who is never off duty for one day and can never retire as long as she reigns. She has one of the loneliest jobs in the world."

Afterward Mother gave me the blue hat that she had worn

to the Palace that day. It is now a permanent exhibit at the Theatre Museum in Boothbay, Maine.

Mother stayed in *The Rivals* until an offer came from Cram Films to make *Arabella* in Italy. At her final performance, when she left the stage in her sedan chair, little did she realize that it was in fact her finale in the legitimate theater. It was a glorious exit.

The thought of working in Italy excited both Magaret and Stringer. "Will this be our third or fourth working honeymoon?" Father asked. Besides, she was rather unhappy with the critical reception to *The Kidnapping of Mary Smith,* a television play in which she had appeared, with John Bonney as the young man. By what they wrote, the critics wanted *their* Margaret Rutherford in comedy, not in a serious play. Fortunately the audience was more understanding and from the letters of a hundred readers praising it, the *Radio Times* printed the following:

> How much I enjoyed *The Kidnapping of Mary Smith.* In addition to the delightful performance given by Margaret Rutherford, what a treat it was to see something other than killings and sex.
>
> (Mrs) M. Y.

> I have seldom been more entertained. This was a complete and happy story, with no obscure meaning, and the acting of Margaret Rutherford and John Bonney was superb—a joy to watch.
>
> (Mrs) P. C.

> Don't take any notice of the critics. They have *no* idea what the public wants. *The Kidnapping of Mary Smith* was just right.
>
> A. P. D.

Father called *Arabella* "the film in which Margaret wore all of those beautiful clothes." As an aging princess she was ably supported by the Italian actress Virna Lisi, whose "beautiful manners" impressed her, and that most British of men, Terry Thomas. Poor Father found himself somewhat surprisingly cast as an Italian gardener complete with wheelbarrow and red neckerchief!

Life in Italy was not easy for either of them, although the Villa Fiorio set in the Frascati Hills outside of Rome was particularly beautiful. Nobody seemed to speak English and they could not speak Italian. "There was the question of our early morning tea, without which I cannot move my legs," Mother complained. "We never did get our tea at the hour we most needed it and sometimes they sent it in a teapot big enough for a family of eight!" As for their bacon and eggs, that situation was even worse. "We got eggs and ham in every form but seldom plain as we were used to having."

They both felt rather ungracious when Consorzio Stampa Cinematografica presented Mother with a medal called "A Life for the Cinema." The ceremony took place at the Brigadoon nightclub in Rome, where Mother wore her best polkadotted plum silk dress, created by Worth. Wrinkling her three chins in her inimitable manner, she thanked the gathering. "Gracia, Consorzio Stampa Cinematografica," she said in faultless Italian, at which her Roman hosts began to cheer.

Returning to Elm Close for a few weeks of rest, my parents were back in Rome that October for dubbing. Two days later mother fell in her hotel bedroom and broke her hip. X rays were taken at the Salvator Mundi Hospital, where the doctors begged her to stay quietly with her hip in plaster for a month. "If only we had listened," Father was to lament so many times afterward.

"I was determined to come home," Mother said. She was flown back to London, being carried on and off the plane by stretcher. On November 7, 1967, London's *Daily Mirror* duly reported the following:

OPERATION FOR DAME MARGARET
Veteran actress Dame Margaret was in "great spirits"

last night after an operation for a fractured thigh bone.

Miss Rutherford, 75, slipped on a rug and fractured her thigh at a hotel near Rome where she was staying last week.

She and her husband, Mr. Stringer Davis, flew back to England, so that the operation could be performed in this country.

When it was suggested that she might sue the hotel for negligence, Mother disdainfully said: "That would be most ungracious." From the London nursing home where she recuperated she made several trips in a wheelchair to the Denham Studios, where the ill-fated dubbing was finally accomplished.

Robert Morley recalls that once Mother was on the way to what she hoped would be a full recovery, she continued to want to work. He says:

> Margaret decided to play a part in a film of Melba in which I was also being paid to appear. Whether it was the script or the ambiance on the set or the fact that she had not recovered from a bad fall, she chickened out on the first day's shooting and the director or one of his aides besought my help to persuade her to continue or rather commence her role.
>
> "Nonsense," I told them, "she doesn't want to do it and you or I would be quite wrong to try and persuade her."
>
> "But, didn't you," he pressed me, "once before get her to change her mind? Have you read the *Nunc Dimittis* [Lord, now lettest Thy servant depart in peace] lately?" I asked.

Robert Morley probably understood Mother's moods as an actress more than any man during her long career, even Father. Father was like me, always the eternal optimist, believing that the impossible could always be accomplished; that one day, as always before, the battle would be won and things would get better.

·9·

The Mother-in-Law

> Observe me, Sir Anthony. I would by no means wish
> a daughter of mine to be a progeny of learning.
>
> Mrs. Malaprop in Richard
Sheridan's The Rivals

T HINGS were not good at Elm Close. Father wrote complaining: "We are very lonely. Where are all the people?" The fact was that even old friends could not bear to see Margaret Rutherford crippled and on two canes.

All the time he clung to the futile dream that she would overcome her latest affliction, as she had all of the mental breakdowns, but it was not to be. She fought a long and gallant battle that I feel, in her dear heart, she knew could not be won.

John Carroll was splendid to both of them, like a true son. He was never too busy to sit and talk over old times with her; there was always a bunch of violets he had brought from Covent Garden, set on the table by her chair.

As for me in America, the greatest crisis of my life had begun. I had the awful feeling deep inside that I was about to die, which in a way I was. My current project was Lady Bird (Mrs. Lyndon) Johnson's biography, which I was dedicating to my parents, and there had been several necessary visits to the White House. I liked Lady Bird Johnson because of her conservation and beautification of America programs; I wanted to call the book *She Planted Trees.* I was so anxious to do a good job but, like Mother, was beginning to feel very low and dejected. The White House people were very kind, especially Liz Carpenter, who arranged the appointments. She would welcome me, sitting waiting at her desk with coffee and cake. I once told her: "It's as if the White House had been given back to the American people."

At this time, I underwent physical bodily changes that lead me in desperation to a gynecologist who said quite simply, "I think you already know what I am going to tell you. You are and have always been a woman." He then handed me a paper written by Dr. James F. Glenn, Chief of Urology at Duke University, a happy choice as Duke University was to request Mother's, Father's, and my personal letters and papers. It said:

> Parents of children born with genital defects should not waste a day in having tests done that will lead to the establishment of the child's most suitable sex-identity. The diagnosis and the decision of whether the child should be male or female can be made as early as the first week of life. The younger the better, to prevent the many psychological problems that can arise.

First I had to choose a name for myself, settling for Dawn, which to me was symbolic of a new day, and Pepita, the name of Vita's grandmother, a Spanish gypsy dancer. Mother, when she heard the news—which she took nobly in stride—simply said, "I love Pepita." Father's comment was compassionate. "Never look down on Gordon, who over the years was very brave." I have tried not to forget it.

Mother and Father were wonderful with their loving support, telephoning me long distance at all hours of the day and night, for time was now of no great importance to either of them. They sent flowers, a Christmas pudding that arrived in an advanced state of decomposition, and a padded British dressing gown, which would have cooked me alive in the Charleston heat! They begged me, when it was all over, to come home for good "to the happy seclusion of Elm Close."

They were relieved to know that at least I was in the capable hands of a good nurse, Mary Kaye Hardee.

When it was all over and at least physically I was whole again, I realized how emotionally immature I was. Mother would write:

> My dear Pepita:
> So you have got through the final crisis! I am so glad to know of this. Now you will feel no unwelcome restraint. How right you were to allow your operation and condition to be public, right and brave! You are in the hands of God, and He will have you in His care, as He has done all the time. May you ever be blessed, as indeed you will be.
> Your loving,
> Mother.

She was still having troubles with her hip and leg, for during the winter she had experienced another fall, "which," wrote Father, "put the muscles wrong on her left side, and she was in such pain that we had to withdraw from the *Song of Norway.*" Unknown to me they were in deep financial trouble again and the accountant was suggesting that they sell Elm Close.

"Selling *Elm Close,*" she cried, "would be like tearing a mandrake up by the roots. Work is the answer . . . work . . . work. . . ."

But work was getting beyond her now. She did provide her voice for a cartoon called *The Wacky World of Mother Goose.* It was a gallant gesture but brought in little money.

She continued to have what she called "my little setbacks," which seemed to come every three or four months. Father wrote: "She fights her way out of them to greater strength but they are still very frustrating and back-to-square-one-ish."

Still, Mother fought hard as she had always done. Leaning on canes, she opened a charity bazaar. She gained further strength, and then, as Father said: "We debated whether she can stand up to a film in August, *The Virgin and the Gypsy,* the D. H. Lawrence story. A wonderful script, but she's finding it rather unpleasant. I think she'd win Oscars with it!"

She was never able to make it. How ironic that at long last she was being offered a straight dramatic role and she was too ill to take it.

Meanwhile, in Charleston I was becoming more sure of my new identity every day. There was a deep sense of relief to be whole at last. I bought pretty dresses, yet I was lonely. Fifty-six Society Street with its walled garden was becoming my prison.

I was perhaps easily persuaded to marriage with John-Paul Simmons, later the father of my daughter, Natasha. However, when our engagement was formally announced, all hell broke loose in Charleston. One would have thought that I had two heads! "White society," says Dena Crane in her video presentation of my life, "took the attitude that Dawn had thumbed her nose at them for daring even to contemplate marrying a black man. Pro-British as they liked to believe themselves, with their love for tradition and mahogany furniture, they failed to take into consideration her deeply religious roots in the Church of England." As Mother said at the time: "A man worth lying down with is worth standing up with too."

Mail arrived by the sackful at the mansion on Society Street; some letters kind and some vicious. I had fifteen Bibles from Born-again Christians and rather a nice red leather-bound copy of the Koran from Saudi Arabia, which I sent home to Father as he liked that kind of thing.

In England there were those like my Burgess cousins who were loyal and kind, while others, whose husbands I had clothed and sent money to when they were poor, were cruelly indifferent. "Her Majesty, the Queen, was sympathetic," wrote Mother. Joan Crawford spoke up for me. "The heart knows why," she told Mother, at the same time sending me a bunch of yellow roses and a yellow ribbon for Jackie, my German shepherd, for Joan liked dogs. Helen Hayes wrote me a letter of encouragement as she had when I was twenty-one years old and had written what was called the first inter-racial morality play, *Saraband for a Saint:* "There is no racial or religious prejudice among people in the theater," she said. "The only prejudice is against bad actors, especially successful ones."

Ironically, Mother and Father were on center-stage again after the lonely lethargy of the last few months at Elm Close. Again, well-meaning friends arrived, if only to gossip about their pending son-in-law. "We are starring in a real drama at last," wrote Mother, I thought a little too ecstatically.

While *Newsweek* devoted a whole page to me, ending with the words "she has rocked the Cradle of the Confederacy," meaning Charleston where the Civil War began, *Time* ran a quote that ended up on *Laugh-In* and the *Johnny Carson* show. Said Mother, "Oh, I don't mind Dawn marrying a black man but I do wish that she wasn't marrying a Baptist."

Looking back, I think that they viewed John-Paul rather theatrically like a latter-day *Othello,* or as the kind of African leader that the Tony Benns were fond of entertaining. "Maybe John-Paul *will* look like some exotic African chieftain," she kept telling Father. Later, after meeting him for the first time and being asked by a lady journalist what she thought of him, she replied quite truthfully, "Well, he does have a nice neck!"

The ceremony was to have taken place in the large Baptist church on Charlotte Street but when the black minister received threats that it would be blown up if it did, he backed out with the words: "Well, you don't have to get married; you can always live together." Fortunately a black Methodist minister, the Reverend William Singleton, volunteered his services. "I always was partial to John Wesley" was Mother's comment when we next spoke by phone. She also gave me explicit instructions that there was to be no wedding march. "I want 'The Battle Hymn of the Republic'."

When I went to get the marriage license the day before, there were two file cabinets marked respectively BLACK and WHITE. "Now I suppose we'll have to start a new one for you," said the clerk. The judge who issued the license, Gus Pearlman, was Jewish. "Welcome to the minority," he said "I have always been in the minority."

The wedding took place the next evening in the lower drawing room of my home on Society Street. While police with bomb detectors searched the basement below, Richia Hail, a white lady from Louisiana who had befriended me, was helping me dress. I wore a gown of white lace with a veil held in place by great-grandmother's Spanish mantilla. The street outside was crammed with people of both races. I could hear the shouts of "Nigger lover."

At the last minute a black lawyer, who had promised to give me away but had political ambitions, refused, so my future father-in-law came up to get me.

With John-Paul's little brother Emmett playing, as Mother had requested, "The Battle Hymn of the Republic" on a small gramophone, I walked slowly downstairs to marry the only man I had ever loved.

The sad little ceremony took place in front of a makeshift

altar upon which stood great-grandmother's statue of Saint Teresa of Avila, Saint of Writers. She had traveled a long way from the cloistered Convent of the Decalced Carmelites in Seville. The minister likened John-Paul and me to Isaac and Rebecca.

After it was over, we put through a transatlantic call to Gerrards Cross, even though it was the middle of the night by British time. We did not wake my parents; they were enjoying their bacon and eggs. They gave us their blessing and then Mother asked: "Dear heart, were you married in church?" When I told her no, and the reason, she was silent for a moment, then said: "There is more than one way to skin a cat. . . . I will call the Archbishop of Canterbury."

I have often wondered if she got His Grace out of bed.

Mother had to wait until fall before what, to her, was the all-important question of the Church of England's approval could be remedied. Their personal invitation cards printed with embossed Old English lettering read:

Mr. J. Stringer Davis
and
Dame Margaret Rutherford Davis, O.B.E.,
request the honor of your presence at
the blessing of the marriage of their
adoptive daughter
Dawn Pepita Langley Hall
to
Mr. John-Paul Simmons
at two-thirty o'clock
Sunday afternoon, November the ninth
St. Clement's Church,
Hastings, Sussex
and afterwards at the reception.

We had arrived in England by air, to be whisked through a side door of Heathrow Airport. Everything had been beautifully arranged by Gwen Robyns, the author, who was acting as a liaison-officer for mother. She explained that as Mother was now so frail, everyone thought it best that she greet me privately at the Wardorf Hotel in London instead of publicly at the airport with a battery of news cameras in attendance. We agreed with Miss Robyns that this was very sensible.

For John-Paul, who had never been out of his native Charleston, it all seemed part of a great adventure. My parents were waiting in a private suite. Father still looked very dapper although he seemed to be smoking too much. Ill-health had taken its toll on Mother. She had lost weight and grown smaller. She was older too, although being on canes does seem to age a person more. John-Paul's kind heart and respect for older people really manifested with Mother. They liked each other from the start; in several of the news photographs at the time he is shown holding her hand. He later was to make a folk-art sculpture of her, using concrete as a medium, instead of his usual clay. Sadly he felt bound to depict Mother as he remembered her, with bent legs, leaning on her two canes. In her hands she holds a little bowl, which he said was to hold crumbs for the birds. He remembered how much Father liked feeding them.

Mother had just been voted the best foreign actress in Germany, so one of that country's leading picture magazines, *Neue Revue,* gave us a beautiful luncheon party. The table was decorated with a centerpiece of Cornish anenomes and purple asters.

Next day Mother had a few bones to pick. She had been incensed by some of the cheap tabloid-like sex stories that had been channeled from Charleston to several of the more flamboyant British newspapers. There was tea with the Archbishop of Canterbury, at which John-Paul, drawing on his natural grassroots philosophy, quite delighted His Grace. All this was in direct contrast to a recent editorial in a South

Carolina newspaper that said I had married "an illiterate Negro."

Then came an all-important visit to Dr. Elliot Phipps, a leading Harley Street gynecologist, who, after examining me, declared in a written statement published on the front page of the large Sunday newspaper, *The People:* "In my opinion she has always been a woman and can have children. It is a tragedy that she was wrongly sexed at birth."

That Sunday, in bright sunshine after a night of heavy rain, I drove with John-Paul through the streets of London on the way to Cousin Rosamanda's home in Horam, Sussex, where I was to dress for the second marriage ceremony. On every billboard and in some cases even tied to lamp-posts was my photograph with these words underneath: SHE CAN HAVE CHILDREN!

How I loved Mother that day. "She can have children." What a wedding gift!

John-Paul left for the church resplendent in a black tuxedo with real lace cravat and cuffs. My cousin, Nigel Burgess, the best man, drove him in a little red sports car. I followed later in a London taxi that was gaily bedecked with white silk ribbons. My cousin Patricia's husband, Derek Ivings, gave me away as Father had his hands full with Mother so crippled. I wore a very theatrical gown of golden brocade with large leg-of-mutton sleeves and a train of gold velvet, designed by David Stokes II. As it was such a windy day, the hairdresser had fastened the veil onto my head with the diamond tiara that Mother had worn as the Grand Duchess Gloriana XIII in *Mouse on the Moon*.

St. Clements, a twelfth-century church in the old part of medieval Hastings, was the perfect choice for so happy an occasion. Nestling at the foot of the downs with the castle above, it was like a page from a history book. Unfortunately the London taxi driver did not know his way and we became terribly lost. Down below we could see the town and church while the bells were ringing madly. It was very frustrating. I was forty minutes late!

Our old friend, the Reverend Tom Savins, now rector of Hastings, was waiting at the west door. "We only open this door for V.I.P.'s" was the way he greeted me. His son Philip was there in red cassock and white surplice, carrying the processional cross and followed, to my surprise, by a full choir. "All the choir members and bellringers volunteered their services," Tom told me.

As I walked up the aisle on Derek's arm with Rosy as matron-of-honor holding my train, I saw my parents and was filled with gratitude. Mother was wearing a gown of silvery blue with a hat of blue osprey feathers to match. Father was sporting a white carnation in his buttonhole. They were both lustily singing the processional hymn, "Lead us Heavenly Father, lead us, o'er the world's tempestuous sea." It was an ironic choice after all that we had been through to have each other.

The only catastrophe during the service was the crash when Roger Pain dropped his camera onto the stone pavement, smashing it to smithereens. But Tom had hidden twenty-two press photographers behind the choir screen! Then Mother stopped the service when, forgetting for the moment that she was not on the legitimate stage, she turned right around and faced the congregation.

"Isn't it wonderful," she said, "Oh, isn't it wonderful!"

Margaret Savins arranged the reception at the Alexandria Hotel in St. Leonard's. It was so close to the sea that we could hear the waves. I thought of many bracing walks that Mother and I had taken on the seafront, her cloak and necklace flying out in the breeze.

Mother had placed a little white church on top of the wedding cake, which she had asked Cousin Rosy to make sure had plenty of marzipan and hard white icing.

After it was over we drove back to London, stopping on the way with Len Golas of *The Sunday People,* who was determined that John-Paul should sample some British fish and chips. On top of champagne and cake, as Mother said, "it was a wonder he wasn't sick."

Next day at Elm Close there was a wedding breakfast, which Father cooked himself. Nobody was allowed in the kitchen while he did it. Afterward he took his new son-in-law for a walk in the garden while I stayed indoors with mother. "Oh, I do hope that they like each other," she kept repeating. When they came in John-Paul was carrying a single red rose, which he gave me with a kiss.

"I've been teaching him how to be a background husband," said Father, at the same time giving Mother a knowing wink.

During this last happy period in their lives, Mother's portrait was painted by Michael Noakes, whose commissions have included such famous people as Prince Charles portrayed as Colonel-in-Chief of the Gurkhas. As she was unable to have sittings in his studio, these had to be done at Elm Close, where Father cooked them all "an excellent lunch." John Carroll had persuaded Mother that she should be painted, for which posterity must be thankful. The finished canvas now hangs in the vestibule of the Globe Theatre while a drawing, also by Mr. Noakes, is in the National Portrait Gallery. Still another graces his studio, where he says it is often commented upon by "sitters and other visitors . . . Always in terms of: 'Ah! Margaret Rutherford. Wasn't she splendid'!"

The Globe Theatre portrait of her, wearing a scarlet cloak and sitting in her favorite wing chair in the inglenook, does her full justice. There is a feeling of satisfaction and resignation about it.

Mr. Noakes recalled one of the sitting sessions:

> Stringer took Margaret for a short walk round the garden after lunch; she was well wrapped up in a splendid

cloak. One of the striking things about her, I recall, was that she was smaller and more delicate than one expected from her films, and really rather a pretty person. She had a tranquillity by the time that I knew her, which some elderly people do seem to gain: but perhaps it was always there, even though I know she had had her problems in life.

She was not very mobile by then, of course. In fact after it was all over and I showed the portrait in the Royal Institute of Oil Painters, at that time at 6½ Suffolk Street, just off Trafalgar Square, and when they came to see the Exhibition, the sergeant on the desk and I had to put her in a wheelchair and carry her up the stairs.

I also recall that when I showed them the pictures after I had completed them, for I do not like people seeing work before that point, Stringer—with all the amazingly rich and exciting things that had happened in their lives to draw on—bubbled with excitement, and said that it was the happiest day of his life . . . perhaps it was "our lives." It could not possibly have been remotely true, but it was so modest, I thought; and, at the time, he believed it!

Michael Noakes' summation of my mother's face and features are interesting to compare with the statement made by Angus McBean, the photographer, on British television, December 9, 1982. He said that she "had such an interesting face to photograph."

I returned with my husband to America. Things had not changed in Charleston. The beautiful ceremony that Mother had arranged in England was not reported in the Charleston newspapers.

Mother's health did not improve, but she never lost her concern for my well-being. I had to go into the hospital for a small operation that should have taken four days, but had the misfortune to fall down and cut my right leg, which resulted in blood poisoning and a hospital stay of a month, after which Mother wrote me:

Dear Dawn Pepita:

I am sorry for the infection in your leg and your being kept in hospital longer than you expected. You are so brave, and getting the publisher's work done in spite of everything! But you will soon be home now, and won't that be lovely?

My dear love to John-Paul. He is so far away, but you will soon be together again now, so take courage.

Ever,
Mother

The story of my life was being published in England by Icon Books, whose editor was Patrick Jenkins, an old family friend of Mother and Father's. The publisher paid my fare to England; this time John-Paul stayed in Charleston. Upon arrival I was interviewed by Molly Parkin of *The Sunday Times,* a most interesting lady dressed all in purple. Miss Parkin's article was straight to the point. She spoke of my adoption by "a famous childless couple." On my first meeting with John-Paul she wrote: "She is rich, he is poor. She is an intellectual and an introvert. He is a boisterous exuberant extrovert. He lives by his body, she by her mind."

Then, of our subsequent marriage, Miss Parkin said: "They have suffered incredible victimisation and literally, in Charleston, walk in fear of their lives. . . . Their courage and tenacity and certainly their love survives the ordeals."

Later, when Patrick Jenkins appeared to have lunch with me, he handed me a copy of Charles Greville's column in the London *Daily Mail,* which read: "Dame Margaret Rutherford will today be reunited with her adopted child, Dawn Langley Simmons."

How good it was to get out of the carriage at Gerrards Cross station and to see coals burning in the waiting-room grate. Mrs. Jones, the lady chauffeur, was there to meet me as Father could not leave Mother alone. On arrival at Elm Close I was shocked to see how much more she had failed since the Hastings wedding. That brave soul whose vigorous footsteps had charged through so many plays and films now walked permanently with those two awful canes. Father waited on her hand and foot for they appeared to have no domestic help at all. She could not bear him out of her sight. Even while he was in the bathroom shaving, she was continually calling: "Dear heart, dear heart, where are you?" With all the strain of home nursing, he too had aged visibly.

Good and loyal Gwen Robyns had been helping Mother write her autobiography under great difficulties because Father forbade any mention of the family murder and of Mother's recurring mental sickness. Gwen was the epitome of patience, even in the middle of the night when Father rapped on her bedroom door with the announcement that it was "eggs and bacon time."

I will always be grateful for those last peaceful days spent in our beloved Elm Close. There was that beautiful feeling of being truly wanted by both of them. Father even accompanied me to a little shop in Gerrards Cross to choose a dress (of a pretty shade of blue) for the autographing party of my new book, *Man Into Woman,* which was to be held in a London hotel. It being one of Mother's "good" days, she was able to go with us to the party. Mrs. Jones drove us.

During our last Sunday afternoon together, while they both took a nap, I walked into the village past stately old elms and holly hedges. It was hard to believe then that the terrors of Charleston had ever existed. I bought a little fluffy toy Easter chicken for Mother and one for the new baby, for Natasha was then on the way. She still has her pre-natal chicken in our china cabinet.

The night before, Mother had become very upset during supper as I kept turning and looking at the windows, whose curtains were not drawn. "Is something the matter?" she asked. The words just seemed to come out of my mouth, and I started to cry.

"I keep forgetting I'm not back in Charleston. I'm afraid of being shot." They both tried to comfort me; all three of us were weeping now.

On the Sunday evening, while Father was pottering in his beloved kitchen, I sat with Mother in the inglenook where Oscar and Ivor Novello's portrait looked down on us. There was a nice little fire of coals and logs burning in the grate. Suddenly Mother, her mind still very alert, picked up a small volume. It contained poetry by Mary Wilson, the wife of a former British prime minister, Harold Wilson. "I'm going to read you my favorite, and I want you to remember the words always," Mother said. Then in her lovely voice, softer from long months of sickness, she began:

> *If I must die, as die I must*
> *First let me fully live,*
> *And grasp and hold a thousand joys,*
> *And take as well as give.*
>
> *And let no experience miss,*
> *But taste and savour all,*
> *And dance throughout the dazzling day*
> *On which the dark will fall.*
>
> *And may the pattern of my life*
> *Lie strand on scarlet strand*
> *'Til God leans from his sapphire throne—*
> *The hour-glass in His hand.*

I have remembered it many times since.

I returned to John-Paul in Charleston, where the fight to save our home on Society Street now began in earnest. When the bank threatened foreclosure of a mortgage they held on the gallery part of the property, restored to house Cousin Isabel's watercolors, I tried to find a buyer so that we would at least receive a fair price. A man from Virginia was definitely interested and returned home to fetch his wife so that she might view the house. Before they could get back, the mansion was sold on the steps of the courthouse just as John-Paul's slave ancestors had been sold so many years before. We had twelve hours to vacate the property. John-Paul and I had moved into a derelict house with seventeen broken windows. We were grateful to have a roof over our heads and hoped now that the white aristocracy would leave us alone. Charleston was his birthplace and he did not wish to leave.

Things were little better at Elm Close, where Mother and Father were in terrible financial difficulties. I sold my Washington Allston painting to the Museum of Southern Decorative Arts in North Carolina to help my parents, but it was not enough. My parents were forced to sell their beloved home and buy a small bungalow a few miles away at Chalfont St. Peter, called Hatfield. Father wrote me: "Yesterday was quite a climactic day. I got off both contracts for the sale of Elm Close and the purchase of our new bungalow near here BY RETURN OF POST with all the deposit-finding-bank-overdraft-problems skirted! My solicitors [lawyers] will be purring with content."

Moving presented a great problem as neither could bear to relinquish any of their treasures. Cramming everything into a small bungalow was practically impossible. Even the garage was filled to overflowing. They still had their moments of happiness, such as receiving a letter from Jan van Lindt, a Dutchman of forty-eight, who began, "Dear Lady, . . . I remember one of your nice films in which you said to the tulips and birds, 'Good morning.' " Mother told Father to save it with other important letters and documents in Aunt Bessie's streamer trunk.

She was soon back in hospital again, where the then Prime Minister, Edward Heath, visited her bedside, a great honor indeed. Dame Flora Robson, describing the occasion, says: "Edward Heath, Prime Minister at the time, called to see her in Gerrards Cross, when she was in an expensive private hospital. She was always so generous with her money; she was running short. Heath took her two thousand pounds from the Civil List, which is only given to those who have done a great deal for the Community."

Father was most unhappy, complaining in a letter to me:

> Although the physical side of your Mother's recovery seemed to be slow but sure, mentally and psychologically we have both had much to stand up to. I have been driven nearly crazy by NOBODY TELLING ME ANYTHING and my doctor NEVER getting in touch with me. At last I declared NEAR WAR on the SISTER! This had come to a HEAD and, this morning, I AM ACTUALLY GRANTED AN APPOINTMENT WITH THE DOCTOR AND MARGARET TOGETHER.

They were both delighted with the news that our daughter, Natasha Margienell Manigault Simmons, had been born on my birthday, October 16, 1971. She had brown hair like mine and was the fourth generation of females in the Hall family to have the family birthmark, a mole on one of her feet. Mother dictated a message for me to Father that said: "One day, your child and our grandchild will grow up to be a leader of her father's people." After that the letters came only from Father.

She was able to come home to the bungalow for a spell and on fine days he would take her for walks in a wheelchair. The neighborhood children were particularly kind to them. He never quite lost his sense of humor, being able to write me: "Today I engaged two lesbian nurses. They can lift your Mother in and out of their little car with ease and take her for rides."

He still fussed that more people didn't come to see them. "ALL our friends now seem to be OLD and hampered too!" he complained. On April 12, 1972, he wrote: "Your Mother is not reading or writing and only talking a little. We are longing to see you both walk down our garden path with our granddaughter."

One special visitor did go to the hospital—Robert Morley. He remembers:

> My last visit to Margaret's bedside was shortly before her death when she was strangely troubled and unhappy and naturally didn't have any idea who I was. She had an unhappy last few weeks but a very happy and fulfilled life before that. She was for a long time the safest box office bet in the business and she knew it, the dear old bird.

On May 22, 1972, my Mother died. She was eighty years old. West Grant, my beautician and a close friend (he had named the baby Natasha), phoned to tell me of her passing, which had just been announced on the radio. Father's cable arrived an hour later. I was devastated. As I could not leave the baby with safety and there was no time to get her name written into my passport so that she could travel with me, I could not fly home for the funeral. Putting on a black dress, I pushed Natasha in the baby carriage to little Shiloh Church where her father's people worshipped. There I sat in an empty pew while she slept peacefully in my lap. Somehow, then, Mother seemed very near.

Messages of sympathy poured in to the bungalow at Chalfont St. Peter and the broken-down house on Thomas Street in Charleston from all over the world. I had over three thousand! Mother, now the perpetual *blithe spirit,* the two words she had directed be carved upon her tombstone "of red Cornish granite because I fought a duel there," would have been pleased with the letter I received from Pauline Saltzman, an American writer on ghostly phenomena: "I realize now that I have never cared for some of her films: I just cared about *her!*"

Writing in the *New York Times* on May 23, 1972, Alden Whitman said:

Creator of a notable gallery of film and stage eccentrics, Dame Margaret Rutherford was a comedienne with few peers who attained stardom in middle age as a result of granitic persistence in sharpening her acting talents.

Film critic Rex Reed fondly wrote: "Margaret Rutherford died, ending a love affair with Miss Marple movies. . . ."

Father received a letter from Prime Minister Edward Heath, and another from former Labour Prime Minister Harold Wilson. Mother, it seemed, was somewhat like the Queen, *above politics*. Wrote Mr. Heath:

> Dame Margaret made an outstanding contribution to the theatre. There must be millions of people who are today remembering her inimitable performances in the theatre, in films and on television and the enjoyment and pleasure which she gave.

Mr. Wilson said:

> For so many years she epitomised all that was best in the British theatre. Her warmth and her talent delighted my wife and me, and countless others, throughout her career.

Father received many other tributes. From the acting profession, C. S. K. Benham, O.B.E. and Chairman of Governors of the Old Vic, remembered that "we at the Old Vic take great pleasure in remembering that it was here she was given the opportunity first to show her great talent before a live audience. . . . It is good to know she never really 'retired' but continued to exercise and give us the benefit of her craft almost to the end of her fruitful life."

David Kossof wrote: "How sad. But she was special and kind, and gave pleasure to many millions. I worked with her only once and the memory is full of her warmth and gentleness."

Dame Flora Robson wondered "if I am the only one who

saw tragedy behind Margaret's brilliant comedy, and I could always see the blue-eyed romantic little girl."

Laurence Olivier remembered the past: "I am so deeply sorry for you in your dreadful, aching loss. . . . She was Beautiful. . . . Your [Father] was very kind to me when I must have seemed boringly much younger than you. I remember that with very much gratitude."

Even in his sorrow, Father could still think of the feelings of others. Binkie Beaumont wrote from H. M. Tennent, Ltd., "I am so deeply sad to learn the news this morning. However I am so grateful to you for having the wonderful thought of letting me be spared the shock of seeing the newspapers."

Writing from the House of Commons, Cousin Tony Benn summed up the family's loss: "I hope that the fact that the whole world is sharing your bereavement will be a comfort at the moment."

It was a personal comfort to me that at the funeral service held in St. James Church, Gerrards Cross, Mother's old co-star and dear friend, Robert Morley, paid her a tribute, dwelling on her life as a fine actress and human being. Dame Flora recalls Father as "he wept alone in a front seat." The service was conducted by the Reverend Canon J. Gordon Harrison, M.A., Vicar of Gerrards Cross, who had enjoyed Mother's buttered scones so much.

Robert Eddison read Henry Vaughan's *They Are All Gone into the World of Light.* Father chose as the hymns "The Lord's My Shepherd, I'll Not Want," and one of my happy Hastings wedding hymns, "Love Divine, All Loves Excelling." As they carried Mother's coffin out into the churchyard, the choir softly chanted the Nunc Dimittis, "Lord, now lettest thou thy servant depart in peace."

She was laid to rest under an enormous blue Colorado spruce.

·10·
Final Curtain: Father

NOT all of the people in Charleston were unfriendly. Finally Natasha's name had been added to my passport so that we could go home to see Father, and as I waited at the airport for the plane that would take me to New York en route for London, fellow passengers General and Mrs. Mark Clark took turns holding the baby for me. We talked of my parents' both being movie stars, and the General told me that his daughter had once dated a handsome actor named Ronald Reagan.

When we got off the train at Gerrards Cross, we were met by Mrs. Jones, who was to drive us to Chalfont St. Peter. "Thank God you have come," she said, obviously very agitated, "Mr. Davis has been to meet the train three times already this morning. He cries and cries."

Father was weeping when we arrived. I noticed the frayed shirtcuffs and the unshaven face. Piles of books, clothing, and motley possessions were everywhere. He was very pleased at seeing Natasha for the first time. We laid her gently on the carpet while we sat on the floor sorting manuscripts and movie scripts that Father thought should go to Duke University, which was making a collection of our joint papers. We decided to give two of the Miss Marple capes to the Victoria and Albert Museum and another to the Theatre Museum in Boothbay, Maine. Then we went to the churchyard.

The tombstone had not then been erected, but the new grave was planted with blue lobelia. Father began to cry again and said between sobs: "I buried her here so that the American pilgrims might also come."

As I had a publishing appointment in connection with *All For Love,* a paperback I had written about my marriage to John-Paul, it was necessary to return to London for the night. Father's clocks had all stopped and we nearly missed the train. As it was, he had to hail a passing police car to get us to the station. We arrived to find the train already at the platform, but when the engine driver recognized Father, he graciously waited for us. Father dropped to one knee as if in some long-forgotten medieval play and doffed an invisible cap. In return, the engine driver raised his hand in a smart military salute.

In the weeks that followed, Father's spirits rallied visibly. He even carried on a lively correspondence with Dame Sybil Thorndike, the veteran actress. Her husband, Louis Casson, had recently died. Sybil and Father found a mutual bond in discussing life after death.

Wrote Dame Sybil: "God rest her, the darling woman— Oh! Stringer, I do so wonder where they are—our beloveds—Are they near us—I do hope so."

Father's last public appearance was at Natasha's baptism, performed by our old and cherished friend, Tom Savins at St.

Clement's, Hastings, on September 17, 1972. Some mischievous spirit must have been present when the baby kicked off her silk shoe into the font!

Father Stringer really enjoyed facing the cameras again outside the church. He had arrived carrying an unwrapped silver christening cup with Natasha's name engraved in Old English lettering upon it. On an envelope he had carefully written:

FOR THE LATE DAME MARGARET RUTHERFORD, O.B.E.
This is surely one day when dear Mother and Father can be with Natasha, you [Dawn] and please God, John-Paul, in the Love of the Lord.

He always remembered his son-in-law.

The bells were pealing as a battery of press photographers took our pictures with the baby, respendent in her traditional white satin Charleston bonnet. Father had fattened me up on his mutton chops, a fact that was clearly visible in the resulting pictures.

After the reception in Eastbourne I kissed him goodbye and he hurried off to his train. I never saw him again, for Natasha and I had to leave next morning for our own home in America. On August 7, 1973, Father died in his sleep, a treasured letter from fellow actor Sir John Gielgud in his pajama pocket. It was buried with him. We never knew the contents.

Remembering him, Robert Morley says:

> I don't think I can subscribe to your view that Stringer sacrificed his career for Margaret. Unkind critics (of which I fear, I was one) found his devotion and protection too good to be true, but on reflection I think I misjudged him as he certainly died of a broken heart once she was gone.

Final Curtain: Father

As Father's coffin was gently lowered beside Mother's, Gwen Robyns said she thought, "I can just hear Margaret saying, 'Hurry up, dear heart, the cream puffs are awfully good up here'!"

·Postscript·

WRITING Mother's story was helped tremendously by the discovery of Aunt Bessie's steamer trunk crammed full of old letters, documents, and photographs. It happened through the strangest of circumstances. In June 1980 I dreamed on three consecutive nights that Father and Mother came to me. Each time Father kept repeating: "The trunk is in the garage . . . the trunk is in the garage." On the third occasion I awoke screaming, with Natasha, then nine years old, slapping my face, for the poor child thought that I was having a heart attack!

I was so upset that I sat down and sent an airmail letter addressed simply to the occupant of our old bungalow at Chalfont St. Peter, asking if there was anything left of our family's residence there. Back came a letter saying that indeed there was, "an old trunk filled with letters and photographs in the garage"!

Shelley Power, then my London literary agent, hurried

down to Chalfont St. Peter were she found a gold mine of information, including letters from two British prime ministers, all the wartime love letters exchanged by my parents, letters from such fellow performers as Lord Olivier, Dame Sybil Thorndike, and Dame Flora Robson, and perhaps most important, data pertaining to the ill-fated William Rutherford Benn.

Dame Sybil would have been very intrigued with this proof of life after death!

·Selected Bibliography·

BOLITHO, HECTOR. *Marie Tempest*. Philadelphia: Lippincott, 1937.

GUTHRIE, TYRONE. *In Various Directions*. New York: Macmillan, 1955.

KEOWN, ERIC. *Margaret Rutherford*. New York: Macmillan, N.D.

OSBORNE, ROBERT, *Academy Awards Illustrated*. Foreword by Bette Davis. Los Angeles: ESE, 1969.

RUTHERFORD, MARGARET, with Gwen Robyns, *An Autobiography*. London: W. H. Allen, 1972.

SIMMONS, DAWN LANGLEY. *All for Love*. London: W. H. Allen, 1975.

SIMMONS, DAWN LANGLEY. "My Mother and the Supernatural." Article in *Fate* magazine, Chicago, May 1981.

TERROT, CHARLES. *An Alligator Named Daisy*. New York: E. P. Dutton, 1955.

·*Acknowledgments*·

I WOULD like to thank Gwen Robyns for her unswerving loyalty to my parents and to me; Adeline V. Muller for encouragement when the days were dark; Anthony Wedgwood Benn, his wife, Caroline, and Timothy Benn for their sincere help; Frank Harmon of the *Cincinnati Enquirer* library; the William Perkins Library at Duke University for use of the Collected Papers of Dame Margaret Rutherford, Stringer Davis, Marjorie Hall Copper, and Dawn Langley Simmons; Rumer Godden; Pauline Saltzman, Dame Flora Robson; Lord Laurence Olivier; Michael Noakes, P. P. R. O. I., R. P.; the National Portrait Gallery, London; the Reverend Thomas Savins, formerly rector of Hastings, and his wife, Margaret; Philip Savins; Gerty Lysaght Dunstall; Dena Crane for valuable research; Barry Brown, Executive Producer, Presentation Programmer, BBC/TV; Liz Smith, columnist, *New York Daily News;* Franklyn Lenthall, curator, the Theatre Museum, Boothbay, Maine; the Victoria and Albert Museum; Amanda Girling; Dr. Jean-Louis Brindamour; Mary M. Rider, Reference Librarian, the Cincinnati Historical Society; The Librarian and Staff, Hudson City Library, N.Y.; The

Acknowledgments

Librarian and Staff, Catskill Public Library, N.Y.; Jay Garon; Rex Reed; Walter Kerr; Alex McIntosh, BBC; Walter Clemons; Joan Sinar, County Archivist, Derbyshire County Council; Patricia Bone; Jim Moseley; Richia Atkinson Hail; Vicky Pont; Patricia Hollowbread for helpful research; Burton G. Harriott; the Reverend Canon J. Gordon Harrison, M.A., Vicar of Gerrards Cross; James Mason; Ronald Harwood; Roger and Vicky Pain; Nancy O. Basey; The Humanties Research Center, the University of Texas, for use of Carson McCullers' letters; Tom Snyder; Marna Anderson; Helen Moore; Jean de Luca; Bea Howe; West Grant; Raymond Bissett; Elizabeth Boice, Women's Editor, *The Catskill Daily Mail;* Martha Pettibon Hundley, writer for the *Nevada Daily Mail;* the Reverend Joseph Simmons; Peter and Marie Schwerin; Nurse Mary Kaye Hardee; General and Mrs. Mark Clark; John Garnier; Lady Fisher; Larry Shelton; my Godmother, Dorrie Humphrey, and her husband, Charles; Louise Profera Wills; the late Evelyn Bernell; James and Rosabelle Waite; James Fickling (Mr. James, the butler); my cousins, Monica Eaglesham, Nigel and Maureen Burgess, Sally Burgess, Peter and Jean Burgess, Patricia and Derek Ivings, David and Midge Chisolm and Alex Kalinowsky; my uncle and aunt, Ernest and Babs Burgess; Nicholas Kostis; Marion Foster; Heather-Rosa Iandola; Jim-Henry Motsinger; Anthony Dawson; Doris Winckler; Edwin Peacock; Irene Carr and the Aaron Burr Bookship, Albany, N.Y., for valuable research; *The Buckinghamshire Advertiser; The Sussex Express and County Herald;* Walter E. Conger, curator, The White House, Washington, D.C.; Walter Henshall; Lucy Griffiths; Dr. Malcolm Troup; Canadian Information Services, Ottawa; the British Information Services, New York; the Danish Information Services; John and Laura Stevenson; Mary Margaret Fuller, Managing Editor, FATE magazine; Barbara Brice McMullin, Regent, Hendrick Hudson Chapter, NSDAR; Barbara Newcombe; Otto Zausmer of the *Boston Globe;* Danny Taylorson; Walter Henshaw; Mary Wilson (Lady Wilson) for kind permission to use her poem, "The Hedonist"; Rosemary Hutton; Max Morgan Witts; Pierre Berton; Peter Bonelli, Advertising Coordinator, British Airways; Betty Pemberton; Paul Trig; Anthony Peek, Royal Haymarket Theatre; Susan Lalor; The Canada Council, Ottawa; S. Purse, Librarian, Canadian Consulate General, New

Acknowledgments

York City; Dianne H. Pilgrim, Curator, the Brooklyn Museum; Mrs. John Hay Whitney; Lady Antonia Fraser; Ita Buttrose, Editor-in-Chief, *The Daily Telegraph* and *The Sunday Telegraph,* Sydney, Australia; Dorothy Jenner, writing as Andrea of *Truth* magazine, Australia; Elfrida Down Kettleborough; Laura Romak; Barbara Holdridge; Hyman J. Fechter; Herman Schindler; Gordon Usticke; Jean Morton, Producer, *Women Today,* ATV; Madeleine McDougal; Mr. and Mrs. G. A. George; Dora Seimons; Beryl Allen; Suellen Austin; and special thanks to my editor Lou Ashworth, her editorial assistant Lisa Grotheer, and my agent, Bobbe Siegel.

·Index·

Index

Index

Index

Index